PRAISE FOR *THE LEMONADE LIFE*

"Practical, heartfelt, simple wisdom for people at any stage of their career (or life)."
—Seth Godin, *New York Times* bestselling
author of *This Is Marketing*

"Zack Friedman is an inspirational leader for the next generation. In *The Lemonade Life*, Zack shows you clearly how to change your perspectives, behaviors, and actions to lead your life with greater purpose. If you want to experience powerful transformation, read this book."
—Marshall Goldsmith, #1 *New York Times*
bestselling author of *Triggers*, *MOJO*, and
What Got You Here Won't Get You There

"Research is clear that mindset and believing your behavior matters have a huge impact on your long-term success. Through stories and ideas, *The Lemonade Life* continually teaches your brain that change is possible if you remain positive and experiment with life."
—Shawn Achor, *New York Times* bestselling author
of *Big Potential* and *The Happiness Advantage*

"Change starts with a change in perspective. Easily said, but not easily done. Zack Friedman shows us how to make lasting change in *The Lemonade Life*, a book rich in encouragement and practical advice. *The Lemonade Life* is a game changer."
—Beth Comstock, author of *Imagine It
Forward* and former Vice Chair, GE

"Zack Friedman has the mind of Tim Ferriss and the passion of Gary Vaynerchuk. *The Lemonade Life* is the must-read book of the year for entrepreneurs and leaders. It will change the way you see the world."
—Brian Roberts, CFO, Lyft

"Zack Friedman's new book, *The Lemonade Life*, is an immensely readable blueprint for finding that elusive pathway that leads to success and happiness. Unlike so many other books, Zack gives us specific things to start to do tomorrow and the next day to get on the road to the Lemonade Life."
—David S. Pottruck, former CEO of
Charles Schwab and *New York Times*
bestselling author of *Stacking the Deck*

"The message of *The Lemonade Life* resonates loudly with me: 'everyone has a shot at greatness.' Other books speak at you; Zack Friedman's book speaks to you. *The Lemonade Life* is thought-provoking, engaging, and compelling reading for anyone who seeks positive change."

—David Novak, cofounder and retired Chairman &
CEO, Yum! Brands; CEO, oGoLead; author of the
#1 *New York Times* bestseller *Taking People with You*

The Lemonade Life

the
lemonade
life

HOW TO FUEL SUCCESS,
CREATE HAPPINESS,
AND CONQUER ANYTHING

ZACK FRIEDMAN

HarperCollins
Leadership

AN IMPRINT OF HarperCollins

Published by HarperCollins Leadership, an imprint of HarperCollins Focus LLC.

Any internet addresses, phone numbers, or company or product information printed in this book are offered as a resource and are not intended in any way to be or to imply an endorsement by HarperCollins Leadership, nor does HarperCollins Leadership vouch for the existence, content, or services of these sites, phone numbers, companies, or products beyond the life of this book.

ISBN 978-1-4002-1160-9 (Ebook)
ISBN 978-1-4002-1159-3 (HC)

Library of Congress Cataloging-in-Publication Data

Names: Friedman, Zack, 1978-author.
Title: The lemonade life: how to fuel success, create happiness, and conquer anything / by Zack Friedman.
Description: New York: HarperCollins, [2019] | Includes bibliographical references and index.
Identifiers: LCCN 2018051109 (print) | LCCN 2018052058 (ebook) | ISBN 9781400211609 (ebook) | ISBN 9781400211593 (hardcover)
Subjects: LCSH: Success. | Success in business. | Self-realization.
Classification: LCC BF637.S8 (ebook) | LCC BF637.S8 F66725 2019 (print) | DDC 158—dc23
LC record available at https://lccn.loc.gov/2018051109

Printed in the United States of America
19 20 21 22 23   LSC   10 9 8 7 6 5 4 3 2 1

To Sarah, Charlie, and Drew—
my sunshine and lemonade

PREFACE

STOP! DO NOT READ THIS BOOK IF . . .

Your life is perfect, and you don't need to change a thing.
You're looking to get rich overnight.
You expect life's problems to go away tomorrow morning.
You prefer style over substance.
You can't do five simple things.
You don't like lemonade.

CONTENTS

SWITCH #5: M IS FOR MOTION

CONCLUSION: Lead the Lemonade Life

Control your own destiny
or someone else will.

—Jack Welch

INTRODUCTION: LUNCH WITH WARREN BUFFETT

Eat like a six-year-old

It's 12:35 p.m. in Omaha, Nebraska, and I'm having lunch with Warren Buffett. We are eating at Piccolo's, which is one of Buffett's favorite restaurants and where he and Bill Gates also have dined together. Somehow, Buffett's root beer float is significantly taller, but it goes with the territory. After all, we're on his home turf, and he's Warren Buffett.

In 2016, a bidder on eBay paid $3,456,789 to have lunch with the Oracle of Omaha. Today, Buffett is picking up the tab. Earlier that morning at Berkshire Hathaway's headquarters, Buffett graciously hosted me and my classmates from Wharton Business School. For several hours, he openly and directly answered any question we asked, occasionally injecting his sharp sense of humor.

Pointing to the Coca-Cola products in the back of the room, Buffett quipped, "Berkshire owns a little over 8 percent of Coke, so we get the profit on one out of twelve cans. I don't care whether you drink it, but just open the cans, if you will."

We all sought to absorb Buffett's infinite wisdom, which we expected would be his take on the economy, investing, and business. The more I listened, however, I realized that the real "wisdom" was less about business and more about living your life with purpose, on your terms, with the things you enjoy, like a root beer float.

Buffett expressed immense gratitude for everything he'd accomplished in his lifetime. He is grateful to be alive. He's not trying to impress anyone or be like everyone else. He maximizes his happiness through his work, his charitable giving, his love of bridge, and his legendary junk-food diet, which he has compared to that of a six-year-old. Warren Buffett knows who he is, and he's comfortable being himself.

After lunch, Buffett posed for countless photos. I'm not referring to the standard group shot where everyone lines up in rows, and he steps in the middle at the last second. For what must have taken nearly two hours, he posed for individual pictures with everyone. There were no bodyguards or assistants. He didn't owe us anything. But he couldn't have been kinder or more generous with his time.

At the end of our lunch, Buffett walked to his Cadillac and drove off into the Omaha afternoon.

While a person is unlikely to forget any part of a day spent with Warren Buffett, a few specifics about the man and the way he approaches life will always stand out to me:

He has a sunny outlook. Simply put, Buffett is happy. His long-term outlook on life and business is positive. He's a believer.

An open mind means access to more opportunities.

He takes calculated risks. As a value investor, Buffett adheres to certain principles that have guided his investment decisions and approach to risk. He especially loves the insurance business, which has taught him how to pay out less than he collects.

When you have a set of principles, you already know how to assess risk.

He does his own thing. Warren Buffett is not trying to be anyone other than Warren Buffett. He chose Omaha, not New York, and has lived in the same house since 1958, which he purchased for $31,500. He prefers cheeseburgers and root beer floats. The stock market's day-to-day movements don't worry him; he's playing a long game. He said he'd rather be a paperboy than a CEO.

There is a certain freedom that comes with independence.

He knows what he's good at. Buffett is genuinely good at being an investor, so that's where he has focused his time and energy. Likewise, he doesn't invest in things he doesn't understand.

Life is more efficient when you know who you really are.

He is a workhorse. Make no mistake: Warren Buffett is a workhorse, not a figurehead who shakes hands and gives speeches. He understands the details, does the analysis, and knows his business inside and out. He reached the pinnacle because he did, and continues to do, the work.

There are no shortcuts to greatness, and there is no escaping hard work.

I asked myself why Warren Buffett is so successful. Some may say he got lucky or that times were easier when he was starting out. But financial fortune aside, Warren Buffett is no different from you or me. He is the result of his choices.

Like Warren Buffett's, your life today is the result of choices. Some choices you made, while others were made for you.

What about your life tomorrow?

From the time you wake up to the time you go to sleep, you have an opportunity to define the next day of your life. Every day. That means each day is a new opportunity to choose the life you want. In the next several chapters, we'll discuss in detail how to make better choices that will broaden your perspective, how to take calculated risks, how to break free from the herd mentality, and most importantly, how to inspire action.

This book is about the choices we make every day, both big and small, that dictate the life we lead and the people we become. The power to define your life begins with five simple switches.

Let's see why.

WELCOME TO THE LEMONADE LIFE

Everyone has a shot at greatness

The only person you are destined to become is the person you decide to be.

—Ralph Waldo Emerson

FIVE SWITCHES TO CHANGE YOUR LIFE

Often, we measure life by annual milestones—birthdays, anniversaries, the school year. Another year older. Time for the New Year's resolution. That's great if you want an annual marker to define your life.

Each year, you have at least 365 chances to take control and define your path. Many people ignore this golden opportunity. Why? The reasons are endless: *Life gets in the way. Don't have the money. Working all the time. Busy schedule with the kids. It's too late. I'll do it next year.*

Every day, you're choosing to live one of two lives: the *Lemon Life* or the *Lemonade Life.*

The Lemon Life is about settling for something less than your full potential. When you settle, you don't actively control your life path, and you allow others to shape your destiny. The Lemon Life is accepting your life as it is—the status quo as a permanent state. The Lemon Life is built on excuses, entitlement, chasing, and pretending, instead of actively and substantively making positive changes to reach your desired outcome. It's the difference between an average and an outstanding life.

The Lemon Life
Your past life = Your current life = Your future life

However, there's a better path, where you can define success and never settle again. It's called the Lemonade Life.

The Lemonade Life is about leading life on your terms, with purpose and possibility. Purpose is the underlying inspiration for your journey. Possibility is infinite opportunity. The nexus between purpose and possibility is action. When you lead a life with purpose and possibility, you can proactively overcome any circumstances.

In the Lemonade Life, what you did five years ago, last week, or earlier today is irrelevant to your future path.

The Lemonade Life

Your past life = Your current life ≠ Your future life

This book is about how to stop passively living the Lemon Life, and to start actively leading the Lemonade Life.

Will you choose to make life happen, or will you let life happen to you? Will you engage in the world to create your legacy, or will you sit back and let others define your legacy for you?

Will you live the Lemon Life or the Lemonade Life?

The answer to that question is based on your ability to do five things.

PRISM: How Lemonade Lifers View the World

This book will teach you how five simple changes will empower you to escape the Lemon Life and start leading the Lemonade Life.

Anyone can make these five changes, regardless of where you come from, what you do for a living, or how much money you have. You can think of these changes as five internal light switches. We all have these five switches and when activated, they are the secret to maximize potential, fuel success, and lead a happier life.

Flipping on these five switches will change your outlook and perspective, make you a better decision maker, and give you the power and freedom to control your life. This book will show you how to flip on each switch, so you can start achieving success, unleashing your greatness, and creating unlimited potential.

So, what are the five switches?

The five switches are a P-R-I-S-M, the lens through which Lemonade Lifers, people like Warren Buffett, view the world:

P = Perspective

R = Risk

I = Independence

S = Self-Awareness

M = Motion

When flipped together, these five switches will create purpose and possibility in your life.

When you switch on *perspective*, you change your *opportunities*.

When you switch on *risk*, you change your *decision-making*.

When you switch on *independence*, you change your *freedom*.

When you switch on *self-awareness*, you change your *self-understanding*.

When you switch on *motion*, you change your *circumstances*.

Here's why these five switches can bring such monumental change:

Switch #1: P Is for Perspective

Change your perspective to change your possibilities.

Your perspective is your primary lens. Your perspective sets the tone for, and shapes what's possible in, your life. Too many people are prisoners to a negative perspective but don't even realize it. But when you have a positive perspective, you see opportunities more clearly.

Switch #2: R Is for Risk

Understand the rewards of risk to make better decisions.

The barriers you create for yourself stymie your progress and limit your opportunities. When you remove these internal roadblocks and better understand the relationship between risk and reward, you clear the path to take more calculated risks and have a more fulfilling life.

Switch #3: I Is for Independence

Avoid the herd mentality to gain freedom of choice.

Independence is often lauded as a desired character trait, but too few embrace it. It's safer to run in groups and find comfort and solidarity in the herd. Independence means rejecting common wisdom and daring to stand alone, even if you're wrong. Independence is the freedom to travel your own path, at your pace, and on your terms.

Switch #4: S Is for Self-Awareness

Master yourself to master your life.

When you self-reflect, you see things you *need* to see, not necessarily what you *want* to see. You hear things you *need* to hear, not necessarily what you *want* to hear. Honest feedback provides an accurate diagnosis to better understand yourself, so you can target the necessary changes to optimize your life.

Switch #5: M Is for Motion

Make lemonade to change your circumstances.

When you make lemonade, you work to create the life you want. You can achieve success with the abilities and tools you already have, so long as you use them to enact change.

The people who are most successful, who maximize their potential, and who never settle for something less than their best self, are fundamentally happy. Their secret—the underlying reason why they're happy—is that they flipped these five switches. They're not all world leaders, business titans, professional athletes, or Hollywood phenoms. In many cases, they're everyday people who made an affirmative choice to create the happiness they now enjoy.

At this point, you might be wondering, *How do I flip these five switches?*

We've all heard the old saying that you can't teach an old dog new tricks. You can't change people when they're set in their ways. You can't make them into who you want them to be or who you hope they will become. The habits, behaviors, and opinions people develop over many years are too ingrained to be changed. It's not even worth trying because you can't change a person, right?

Here's the thing: it's only true that you can't teach an old dog new tricks if the dog is unwilling to learn. You can repeat every excuse as to why you can't change, why you won't change, or why it's impossible to change.

You can choose to change, and when you flip these five switches, you'll see your life through a new PRISM, while leading your Lemonade Life.

The bold truth is that no matter what happened before, *today is your day.* Today is the day you take full control of your life.

Yesterday was the last day you said, "I can't."

Today is the first day you say, "I will."

When you understand what it means to be in control of your life, it's an awesome power and responsibility. It's your pathway to greatness. You live in one of the most amazing times in history. It may not feel like the *best* time. It may not feel like the *perfect* time. But right now is the *greatest* time because everyone has a shot to fulfill their destiny. This is your time.

If you're playing against another team—whether it's your friends, your coworkers, your parents, your siblings, or society—you're playing the wrong game. If you think you must attend a certain school, work at a certain job, shop at a certain store, or hang with a certain crowd, you're playing the wrong game. The only game you should be playing is one-on-one. This is you against you. You, and only you, are in control of your life. You're working on yourself. You make your own decisions on your terms. You have the power to decide your future. When you fall into the trap of social comparison, it's a losing game.

In our culture of instant gratification, too many people want outcomes now. They want the shortcuts and output, but they lack the willpower and determination to do the more important work that precedes the outcomes. If you don't have the right mind-set and work ethic to implement these changes, advice is just advice. Too few are willing to do the hard work on themselves. We should be focusing our efforts on the habits we form and the choices we make. This is where it all begins. Our outlook, mentality, principles, and self-understanding guide our decisions. Start with building the proper foundation before you focus on the outcome.

As you read this book, my hope is that your life will change for the better. For some, change may be incremental. For others, it may be monumental. I want this to be your playbook to tackle anything that comes your way, to manage any situation with focus and serenity, and to be happier as you navigate your life. Whether you're reading this book under an umbrella on the beach, in a seat on an airplane, under a tree in the park, standing among the crowd on the subway, on the couch in front of a fireplace, or in bed sipping tea, remember that *today is your day*.

I want you to win. My hope for you is that from this day forward, you'll see yourself and those around you in a new light. If you're not leading the life you want, my hope is that you'll have the courage to stand up and take what's yours. I want you to crush every roadblock and conquer every fear. I want you to reposition your mind and have the conviction to think unconventionally.

The choices you make from this day forward should be for you. Not for anyone else—for you. This is your life. Care for it with the dedication and attention it deserves. You don't need anyone's permission but your own. You have the power to control your destiny if you're willing to put in the work. It won't happen overnight—far from it. This is a lifelong process and journey on which you are about to embark. You must be willing to sacrifice and fight for it. If you haven't yet reached that mountaintop, that's all about to change.

Now is your time to determine who you are and who you want to become. This book is for the successful who want to succeed more. It's for the strugglers who want to struggle less. It's for the dreamers who want action, and for the actors who never stop dreaming. It's for the believers who think anything is possible, and the nonbelievers who don't. It's for the people who are stuck, and for those who are free. It's for those starting their journeys, those who are on their journeys, and those who think they're finished with their journeys. It's for the entrepreneurs who finally want to take the plunge. It's for the hungry hustlers who never quit, and for the quitters who never hustle. It's for anyone who has been told no. It's for everyone who gives but feels that others only take. It's for the tired who need more energy, and for the energetic who are never tired. This book is for anyone who wants more happiness, more greatness, and more fulfillment in life.

This book is for *you*.

If you're willing to make that commitment to yourself, if you're willing to do all that it takes to reach the other side, and if you're willing to put yourself out there to make history, then let's do this.

SWITCH #1

P IS FOR PERSPECTIVE

Change your outlook to change your possibilities

A man is but the product of his thoughts. What he thinks, he becomes.

—Mahatma Gandhi

MEET THE LEMON LIFERS

I want to introduce you to three people you already know.

You've met them before, somehow and somewhere: they are your neighbor, your colleague, a parent at your child's school, a friend of a friend at a backyard barbecue. You've watched them at a cocktail party or at your family reunion. You may know them from the gym or from your book club. You've surely had dinner with them before.

You may even be one of them.

I'm talking about Lemon Lifers. It's easy to spot Lemon Lifers because they are *everywhere*.

There are three main types of Lemon Lifers:

- Eternal Excusers
- Steady Settlers
- Change Chasers

Let's meet them again for the first time.

The Eternal Excuser

Eternal Excusers have endless reasons for why they can never lead the Lemonade Life. It's too much work. It's too much time. It's only for rich people. Their negative mind-set is their own worst enemy. Eternal Excusers spend more time worrying about doing something than actually doing something.

At their core, they are the ultimate complainers. They invented the buzz-kill. They see rain clouds on a sunny day, point out the problems with an offered solution, and usually attribute winning to luck.

From their front-porch rocking chair to the confines of their sofa, action is *not* their middle name. They love to give their opinion, especially when you're not asking for it. They are somehow experts on everything (a.k.a. nothing), but when it's their turn to jump in, they suddenly get cold feet.

Eternal Excusers have expectations about how life "should" be. When those expectations fall short, Eternal Excusers become frustrated. Until they remove their psychological roadblocks and transform their way of thinking, Eternal Excusers cannot lead the Lemonade Life.

Eternal Excuser at a Glance

WHO: Your cynical friend, parent, colleague, or neighbor who could never do *that* because it's just too much time, effort, and money.

TAGLINE: "The system is rigged."

HAPPINESS DERIVATION: Eternal Excusers gain comfort from their "us versus them" cocoon and gain power from criticizing other people, places, and things from the safety of their stoop, balcony, or office watercooler.

FIRST QUESTION AT A BACKYARD BBQ: They don't ask questions because they don't care what you have to say. But they'll be first to respond to your statements with "Yeah, but . . ." or "I would have done that, too, if only . . ."

MOST LIKELY TO TELL YOU: That you have a greater chance of being struck by lightning than winning the lottery. However, they still play the lottery regularly and haven't been struck by lightning (yet).

Eternal Excusers make all types of excuses. Here are the five most common:

Five Most Common Excuses from an Eternal Excuser

Excuse #1: It's too hard.

Eternal Excusers love to quit before the race begins. Since they magnify road-blocks, they make easy tasks hard and hard tasks harder. Everything is more challenging than it needs to be, and the weight of a challenge crushes the Eternal Excuser's spirit. Here's the thing: few things are as hard as they seem. Even if you think something is hard, there's always a solution, and it's up to you to find one.

This excuse is about lack of creativity and determination.

Excuse #2: It takes too much energy.

Eternal Excusers operate on limited energy. They don't approach life with vigor. Molehills seem like mountains, and mountains take substantial energy to climb. Eternal Excusers have more energy than they realize, but they can only unleash it when they understand their full potential.

This excuse is about lack of motivation.

Excuse #3: I didn't go to a good school.

The school you attended or didn't attend isn't the singular predictor of career achievement. Do you know how many millionaires, billionaires, and other successful people didn't go to college, dropped out of college, or didn't attend the "right" school? Eternal Excusers like to find reasons why they can't do something, and lack of formal credentials is an easy excuse on which to rely.

This excuse is about lack of self-appreciation and self-respect.

Excuse #4: I don't know how to do that.

Guess what? Neither does anyone else. Eternal Excusers create knowledge barriers, as if everyone is born knowing everything. Like Bill Gates used to program mainframe computers as a toddler. The biggest myth about smart and successful people is that they know everything. What separates them from Eternal Excusers is that they're not afraid to trust in themselves to do the work to learn more. They're not afraid to admit they don't know everything, or anything, on a given topic. They read, ask questions, take classes, and find a mentor to ensure they level the playing field. In the end, they'll know more than everyone else, even if it didn't start out that way.

This excuse is about lack of trust in yourself.

Excuse #5: It takes too much time.

Eternal Excusers cite time as a common excuse, as if they have so many other things going on in their life that warrant more attention. We all operate in the same confines of a twenty-four-hour day. However, it's how you prioritize your time that counts. Do you value your time? If you want something badly enough, you'll find time to make it happen. You'll rearrange your schedule to give up something to gain something. You'll invest the time, energy, focus, determination, and dedication to reach your destination. Eternal Excusers should ask whether they're devoting the greatest number of hours to the most important things.

This excuse is about lack of prioritization and self-discipline.

Five Signs That You May Be an Eternal Excuser

Now that you know the favorite excuses of an Eternal Excuser, here are five signs to determine if you are one:

It's them, not you.

Everything that happens to you is because of other people. They wronged you in some way. They prevented you from getting what you want.

The problem with this mentality? There's no personal accountability. You don't own up to your role. You don't take responsibility for your actions. It's always someone else's fault. Until you take responsibility for your choices and decisions, the blame game is an easier deflection strategy. It's a defensive posture, so you don't have to carry the burden of real work. The irony is that when you take ownership and admit your faults, that's when the burden is lifted. Accountability is the greatest form of freedom. You have control of your own destiny, and you're responsible for all that results from your actions.

It's easier in the short term to point the finger at others than point it at yourself.

It's impossible for the little guy to win.

It's all rigged. All of it. The stock market. Politics. Your job. They run the world, and you don't. They make all the money, and you don't. They take credit while you get none. They always win, and you always lose. You have no options but to operate in their world.

It's a defeatist attitude, but all too common. This mentality is a losing one. You've diminished your own stature by making yourself the little guy. You've conditioned your mind to believe that you're weaker than you are, slower than you are, and less powerful than you are. Your incessant complaining has stifled your progress, and you've taught yourself to just accept whatever life throws at you. Life is happening to you. You are in a state of receipt, not of taking.

It's not me against the world—it's the world against me.

You like to opine from the sideline.

You have a lot to say about everything. You think you're in the know. You're eager to share your thoughts with anyone who will listen, but those thoughts rarely elevate the target. Rather, you prefer to criticize, comment, or tease. When it's your turn to act, you are quick to decline. It's not your way. You're more behind the scenes.

It's safer to pass judgment from the comfort of the front porch.

You could have but didn't.

Imagine all the things you could have done. Too numerous to count. All those times you were going to start a business. That time you were going back to school. How you planned to go on that around-the-world trip. When you were all ready to move across the country.

Well, times are different now. You're older. There's not enough time. Your schedule is so busy. You're settled. Your day has passed.

If only . . .

Watercoolers are not meant for water.

"Coffee break? You just took one fifteen minutes ago? Oh, come on—let's grab another one."

You can't get enough breaks. In fact, you'll distract yourself with almost anything to get away from working.

"Only five hours and fourteen minutes left until we go home."

Breaks are your happy place. They're your time to unload on management, your coworkers, and your boss. Work isn't really your thing, but you shine during break time. You use your self-anointed role as chief break-taker as your bully pulpit, and the break room as your stage.

It's more fun to talk at work than to do work.

The Steady Settler

Steady Settlers make their bed in a home of complacency. They have followed the path of conventional advice, a path chosen by others—society, friends, parents, or neighbors. Therefore, Steady Settlers are the ultimate conformists: they live someone else's dreams, not their own. On the surface, Steady Settlers may appear action oriented.

However, that doesn't mean they're making meaningful progress toward the life they truly want to lead. Risk averse, Steady Settlers prefer to play it safe. Why? They may not admit it, but they're afraid of the unknown and of failure. Steady Settlers plan "not to lose" rather than to win. They also prefer caution, even when creativity may be demanded.

For many Steady Settlers, appearances are *everything*. They want you to think they have the perfect life. (*Their holiday card helps sell the dream.*) They want you to think they love their job. (*They've been at the same company for fifteen years—"A real lifer through and through."*) They talk frequently about their home or homes. (*"We're in the Hamptons all summer—you should stop by."*) Unlike Eternal Excusers, however, Steady Settlers don't necessarily wear unhappiness on their sleeve. While Steady Settlers want you to think their life is dandy, the truth is they are living a lie, or at least an uneasy compromise.

They work eighty-five hours a week and don't have time to see the 2.5 kids they thought they were supposed to have. It's one thing if they like their job, but they usually don't. They stay there because it gives them a coveted title, pays their huge mortgage, or helps maintain their social status. Many Steady Settlers think they're actively playing the game, but they're drifting through it. They float from one life milestone to the next, afraid to deviate from their path. Their current job was the logical next step; it's what they assumed was expected of them. Since Steady Settlers refuse to leave their comfort zone, they don't take charge of their own destiny and often never achieve their dreams. In this complacent or even artificial life and seemingly endless circle of appearances, Steady Settlers are stuck.

Steady Settler at a Glance

WHO: Your sibling, your classmate, or that parent at your child's school who: (a) can't stand the clients or the hours, but is constantly telling you that you would be crazy to leave the firm; (b) doesn't like this neighborhood but can't understand why you want to move; or (c) would rather be closer to their hometown but is convinced that if you don't work in the New York office, you'll never get the big promotion.

TAGLINE: "I'll have what they're having."

HAPPINESS DERIVATION: Steady Settlers gain satisfaction from the certainty of their comfort zone, even when they can't stand the zone itself. They keep playing even when they don't like the game. They also feel validated in their choices when they have others' approval.

FIRST QUESTION AT A BACKYARD BBQ: "So, where do you work?"

MOST LIKELY TO TELL YOU: The plural of "attorney general" is "attorneys general."

Despite their sources of happiness, Steady Settlers are fundamentally *un*happy (even if they think or say otherwise). However, even if they don't like their job, they do experience annual glee in the form of promotions and financial bonuses. This satisfies their fundamental need for safety and stature.

Steady Settlers are not comfortable with change. That's their primary pitfall. The world around them is evolving, but they're so buried in their cocoon that they miss opportunities and fail to adapt. Steady Settlers can still maintain their family structure, personal identity, core beliefs, and values when they become open to possibilities for change.

Five Signs That You May Be a Steady Settler

Think you may be a Steady Settler? Here are five signs that you are:

Life is one big checklist.

It's like that calendar you keep on your wall, except this is the checklist of life. You check off each accomplishment. You mark every accolade. You note every title acquisition. Even the squeaky sound of removing the cap from your marker creates an adrenaline rush.

As you reach new heights on Mount Résumé, you've invested little time developing the positive habits and skills that should accompany these pursuits. You spend less time learning and experiencing, and more time collecting.

Some people collect art. But my LinkedIn profile is my masterpiece.

Hear ye, hear ye. I present to you, the royal résumé.

Within thirty seconds of meeting someone, you announce, unprompted, to the unwilling participant your job title, employer, and pedigree. You are defined by your career. You want everyone to know what you do, where you work, how you got there, and how it is all fantastic.

So, what do you do for a living?

The kindergarten that your child attends matters.

You can't get into Harvard unless you go to the right high school. You can't go to the right high school unless you go to the right middle school. You can't go to the right middle school unless you go to the right elementary school. You can't go to the right elementary school unless you go to—you guessed it—the right kindergarten.

That's right. It all starts with kindergarten. For some Steady Settlers, it starts even earlier, with the right preschool and even the right day care.

Appearances matter. Yours and your children's.

The admissions committee is watching.

You love (but really despise) your job.

Let's face it. You hate your job, but you keep finding reasons not to do anything about it because leaving the job could mean leaving your lifestyle. Frankly, giving up your job is a terrifying thought.

How else can you possibly pay off your 95 percent loan-to-value mortgage?

The sacrifices we make.

Life is great—really, really great.
No, it's not. You've settled for the life you think others want and don't know how to get out of the endless circle of keeping up appearances. At this time in your life, you're not where you want to be. Maybe this is where your classmates should be, or your childhood friends, but not you. However, you would never admit that to your friends. You fear that you would be laughed at, be ridiculed, and take an unfortunate nosedive in social status.

Many of your friends feel the same way, but like you, they're too scared to share.
I love the Lemon Life.

The Change Chaser

Change Chasers will do anything to improve their life—but there are caveats. They say they crave something more, but they're unwilling to fight for it. They claim they like the destination, but they're unwilling to take the journey. They like the title of "entrepreneur," but they despise the grind.

Unlike Eternal Excusers and Steady Settlers, Change Chasers are risk seekers. While they prefer unconventional approaches, Change Chasers don't invest the necessary time to learn before execution. They are fad finders, trend followers, and impulse buyers, who are focused solely on the ends, not the means. Fear of missing out, or FOMO, is in their DNA.

Change Chaser at a Glance
WHO: Your crazy uncle, pitching yet another get-rich-quick scheme.
TAGLINE: "Herds are meant to be followed."
HAPPINESS DERIVATION: Change Chasers gain comfort and stature from the chase, and making sure they're involved with the latest and greatest.
FIRST QUESTION AT A BACKYARD BBQ: "Wait—did somebody just say 'next big thing'?"
MOST LIKELY TO TELL YOU: How much money they made during the "cash for gold" craze (while conveniently omitting how much they subsequently lost trading digital currencies).

On the surface, Change Chasers appear independent and entrepreneurial. After all, they're on a quest to make money on their own terms. The reality is far different: rather than think independently, they blindly follow fleeting trends. Financial autonomy is a motivation, but the outward projection of financial success is more important. Despite their action-oriented mind-set, Change Chasers rarely finish what they start. When they can't get rich quick, they lose interest and are already searching for the next big thing. They're not closers.

Five Signs That You May Be a Change Chaser

Here are five ways to tell if you are a Change Chaser:

The market is on fire.

"The market is hot. If you don't get in right now, you'll miss out. The time is now, my friends. This won't last forever. We have never seen an opportunity like this one. When you look back twenty years from now, you'll be asking yourself why you weren't a part of this once-in-a-lifetime opportunity."

The good news is that the market is always hot. The bad news is that the market is always hot.

Get 'em while they're hot.

They are literally printing money.

"At every turn, behind every corner, there's money to be made."

Since every opportunity is a good financial opportunity, your investment filter is usually flipped to the off position.

It's like the gold rush all over again.

Get in and get out.

"This isn't going to last forever. The trick is to get in and get out. This isn't a long-term play. There's only a small window of opportunity."

Commitment takes time and effort, and those are two things to which you cannot commit.

People say there's no real way to make a quick buck. This is a real way to make a quick buck.

You invented Uber before Uber invented Uber.

"I created the Cronut®, the fidget spinner, and *The Fresh Prince of Bel-Air* years before anyone else knew who Carlton Banks was."

You have a million ideas but few implemented ones. You are creative but don't do the necessary work to follow through. You love to start projects but don't love to finish them. When the going gets tough, you've already lost interest or moved on.

When I was in seventh grade, I had this idea to put coffee shops on every street corner.

Your risks aren't calculated.

"If you want to win, you need to risk it all."

You think every opportunity warrants a huge bet. You're a big risk taker, but not a calculated risk taker.

Jump, but don't look down.

So here they are: the three people you already know. However, there's a fourth person I'd like you to meet. If the Eternal Excuser, Steady Settler, and Change Chaser are three people you *already* know, this fourth person is someone you *should* know.

3

WHEN LIFE GIVES YOU LEMONS

*H*ow do you share a lemon?

It was the same question I was asked during my first week at Wharton Business School. One lemon, two partners. You can divide it any way you like. How would you do it? What would you choose? Can you reach common ground? What if your ideas are different? What would everyone else do?

The first team divided the lemon down the middle: each partner took half. They followed directions. Simple enough.

The second team peeled the lemon: one partner kept the lemon peel and the other kept the fruit. One partner focused on the core. The other chose the shell.

The third team peeled and split the lemon: one partner kept the seeds, and the other kept the rest. One partner had the fruit. But the other could plant a tree.

But the last team did something unique. They cut the lemon in half, discarded the seeds, and grabbed a half-filled bottle of water. One partner carefully squeezed the lemon halves into the bottle, while the other added sugar left over from his morning coffee run. A few shakes of the bottle later, they held up their creation and said the proverbial line: *"When life gives you lemons, make lemonade."*

The class laughed, but that memory stuck with me. There are many ways to divide a lemon. You can cut it, peel it, pit it, squeeze it. These two students, however, didn't think like everyone else. They weren't limited by their ingredients. They didn't just check the box or copy their neighbor. They did it their way.

They made lemonade.

I want you to meet someone who is just like these students. This person is someone worth meeting, someone you should get to know: the Daring Disruptor.

Daring Disruptor at a Glance

WHO: Daring Disruptors are game changers who drive creativity, innovation, and transformation on their own terms. Original thinkers, they proactively take calculated risks to reach their full potential.

TAGLINE: "Lead the Lemonade Life."

HAPPINESS DERIVATION: Daring Disruptors win because they dare to be bold, succeed because they think unconventionally, achieve because they never stop learning, and excel because they take risks to seize opportunities.

FIRST QUESTION AT A BACKYARD BBQ: "How can I learn more about *you?*"

MOST LIKELY TO TELL YOU: How their morning routine helps set the pace for their day, and that they'll gladly share it, so you, too, can benefit.

Five Morning Routines of a Daring Disruptor

Daring Disruptors don't all follow the same morning routine. If they did, they'd be Steady Settlers or Change Chasers. Eternal Excusers don't bother with morning routines—they'd have to wake up earlier, they don't have the time, and they generally can't be bothered. Daring Disruptors find the morning routine that works best for them. For some it's meditation, for others a jog or a swim. Others make lists of the day's tasks. The goal is to rejuvenate the spirit and clear the mind for the day ahead. Here are five of the best morning routines that Daring Disruptors incorporate into their lives:

Eat a live frog first thing in the morning.

"Eat a live frog first thing in the morning, and nothing worse will happen to you the rest of the day" is paraphrased from Nicolas Chamfort and later credited to Mark Twain. Plan to complete the hardest task of the day first, so you get it over with and can move on to easier tasks. Conquering that initial hurdle will prevent procrastination and make other tasks seem less daunting.

If you don't like eating frogs first thing in the morning, you can do the opposite: save your frog for later in the day. Start your morning with easy tasks you know you can complete. This will enable you to get a few wins and build confidence early, so the harder tasks later won't seem as challenging. According to professors Francesca Gino and Bradley Staats in *Harvard Business Review*, completing smaller tasks first not only is psychologically rewarding, but also can increase your ability to confront tougher challenges later in the day. When you achieve even small goals, as Gino and Staats explain, your brain releases the neurotransmitter dopamine, which can improve attention, memory, and motivation to complete the next task.

Find your unique rhythm and discover what motivates you intrinsically. Identify it, implement it, and stick to it.

Ask yourself: "What good shall I do this day?"

Ben Franklin's favorite morning routine started with him asking, "What good shall I do this day?" Your day doesn't have to be a burden. Find ways you can create good in the world, even if it's a seemingly small contribution. Drop extra money in the tip jar. Put an inspiring note in your child's backpack. Counsel a friend in need. This routine is not only about serving others, but also about creating impact and value.

Better yet, connect this altruistic behavior to your greater life purpose. When you give to others and make a positive contribution to the world, you can create what the Japanese call *ikigai*, which roughly translates to "a life worth living." Researchers employed the Ohsaki Study to ask 43,391 Japanese adults, "Do you have *ikigai* in your life?" After tracking the health of these adults for seven years, researchers found that those without *ikigai* had a significantly higher risk of all-cause mortality compared to those who found *ikigai*.

Think of *ikigai* as your life's purpose. It's your calling and driving force. It's the underlying reason why you do what you do. When you find your ikigai, it's the secret to a happier, more fulfilled, and longer life.

Connect with someone you love.

Start your day with happiness by connecting with someone you love. Have breakfast with your significant other. Hug and kiss your children. Text or call your loved ones and tell them how much they mean to you. Researchers at the University of North Carolina at Chapel Hill found that hugging your partner can reduce your heart rate and blood pressure, which otherwise can be elevated during stress. When you give and receive love as soon as your day starts, you have an extra boost to live your day with purpose.

Write down three things for which you are grateful.

Each morning, spend five minutes writing down three things for which you are grateful. For example, you can write about people you value, your unique personal characteristics, or what you accomplished the previous day. This exercise will ground you, make you feel thankful, and give you a shot of happiness. Researchers have found that journaling about things for which you are grateful, compared with hassles or a neutral topic, can lead to improved mood, feelings of happiness, and positive emotions. When you start your day surrounded by gratitude, it's a breathtaking experience.

Gratitude journaling is one key way to increase happiness and well-being. You can maximize the benefits of gratitude by taking your journaling one step further. Write a thank-you note to a friend, family member, or colleague to tell them how much you appreciate him or her. This could be your friend who assisted with your job search, your cousin who painted your garage, or your coworker who helped you with a presentation. Your writing quality matters less than your sincerity.

Better yet, say thank you face-to-face. According to research from the University of Chicago, expressing gratitude through thank-you notes can increase the well-being of both you and the recipient. Research shows that we underestimate the value of expressing gratitude, while overestimating how awkward the recipient might feel. A separate research study shows that thanking someone mentioned in your gratitude journal for something specific—and then reflecting on your own feelings and the person's reaction—can decrease your negative emotions and make you feel less depressed.

The practice of gratitude offers multiple positive health benefits. According to Robert A. Emmons, a leading scientific expert on the science of gratitude, gratitude "can lower blood pressure, improve immune function . . . facilitate more efficient sleep . . . [reduce] lifetime risk for depression, anxiety and substance abuse disorders, and is a key resiliency factor in the prevention of suicide."

Do what Steve Jobs did.

For his 2005 Stanford commencement address, Steve Jobs shared his morning routine, which had consisted of asking himself one question every morning for the previous thirty-three years:

"'If today were the last day of my life, would I want to do what I am about to do today?' And whenever the answer has been 'no' for too many days in a row, I know I need to change something."

Every morning, you have a choice to do what you want and do what makes you happy. Yes, you'll still have responsibilities, but you get to dictate your path. If you're on the wrong one, you have the power to change your direction. Many people let months and years pass without doing a check-in on their happiness, joy, and fulfillment. Don't let that be you. Check in with yourself every morning.

Now that you've met these four new friends, let's see why only one of them leads the Lemonade Life.

The Lemonade Life: Who Leads It and Why

Access to the Lemonade Life is based on two character traits: (1) whether you follow a conventional or unconventional life path, and (2) whether you are proactive or reactive to change your life circumstances.

Each of the Lemon Lifers can be measured against these two character traits.

- Eternal Excuser: conventional and reactive
- Steady Settler: proactive, but conventional
- Change Chaser: unconventional, but reactive

Without changing their ways, none of these Lemon Lifers will ever lead the Lemonade Life.

To lead the Lemonade Life, you need to be unconventional *and* proactive. That's how the Daring Disruptor operates.

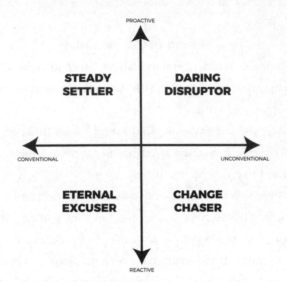

You want to be in the upper right quadrant:

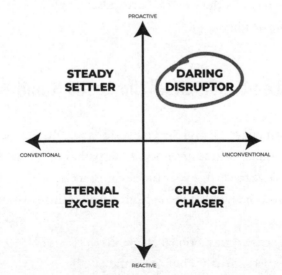

The Daring Disruptor doesn't depend on external things to achieve happiness. For the Daring Disruptor, happiness and fulfillment come from within. They're based on your ability to determine and define your life path, and love the life you choose. I don't want you to think that Lemonade Lifers are happy all the time. They're not. What distinguishes Lemonade Lifers from Lemon Lifers is an innate ability to use the five switches to weather life's storms. Lemonade Lifers, above all, are resilient.

I want you to embrace a fundamental, powerful truth: happiness is a possibility in your life. Your greatest happiness is already inside. You can achieve whatever you want, whenever you want, when you choose to let your happiness out. When you position your mind-set toward purpose and possibility, your ability to experience happiness is infinitely more tangible.

The Power of Give and Get

How do we change our perspective? How do we transform from an Eternal Excuser, Steady Settler, or Change Chaser to a Daring Disruptor? The move is easier than you think, and it all begins with the power of "give and get."

We've all heard of give-and-get relationships. Give some, get some. Do good things, and good things will come back to you. Too many people focus only on the outcomes—what they gain. But success is about what you give up to gain.

I want you to succeed by having a give-and-get relationship with yourself. For everything you give up, you'll gain something in return. Write down five things in your life you want to give up, and then think of the corresponding things you'll gain. This powerful exercise will show you the value of letting go of destructive forces and replacing them with uplifting ones that bring increased confidence and self-discipline.

Let's look at this give-and-get relationship in the context of Lemon Lifers.

Eternal Excuser

Give up	Gain
Excuses	Accountability
Negative outlook	Clearer mind
Complaining	More energy
Blaming	Responsibility
Worrying	Trust in self

If Eternal Excusers stop making excuses, they'll begin to become accountable for their own actions. Accountability doesn't have to be a scary thing. Accountability can be empowering; it means you can gain control over your life. Similarly, when you remove a negative outlook, you open the parameters of your mind. You can think more clearly and openly, which helps you develop a healthier perspective. When you give up complaining, you gain more energy. It's hard to appreciate how much time and effort an Eternal Excuser spends on negative energy, but removing it from your life will free up positive energy to accomplish more productive and rewarding tasks.

Like accountability, taking responsibility for your actions will increase your freedom and independence. When you blame others, you're tied to them in a way. You derive satisfaction from them, even if they're the target of your derision. When you take responsibility for your own actions, you're in charge of your satisfaction, not them. When you fall, you are equally responsible for your mistakes, which only you can correct anyway, so you're better off looking inward for strength.

Finally, when you give up worrying, you empower yourself. Worrying means you don't trust yourself enough to take a step forward. You don't trust that you can stand back up if you trip and fall. When you give up worrying for good, you'll gain trust in yourself, your abilities, and your actions.

Now, let's move on to the Steady Settler.

Steady Settler

Give up	Gain
Settling	Possibility
Risk aversion	Opportunity

Caution	Creativity
Convention	Independence
Closed-mindedness	Adaptability

When Steady Settlers stop settling, they open a whole new world of possibility in their lives. Settling is about cutting your life short and not reaching your true potential. It's about erecting artificial barriers that inhibit progress before you have begun your real journey. Steady Settlers stop before they reach the pinnacle because they mistakenly think they've already arrived. Their lives are constructed in a riskless vacuum covered in a false sense of security. When they give up a riskless existence, they gain opportunity. This opportunity creates new pathways to achieve more in their life. When Steady Settlers focus more on possibility, it's a powerful platform to lift them from self-imposed mediocrity.

Steady Settlers remain overly cautious, which isn't a matter of personal safety or security. It's a mind-set and perspective ingrained in their psyche. It's also an excuse to avoid expanding their worldview. When Steady Settlers give up caution, they gain creativity. That creativity can help them access new opportunities, solve problems more quickly, and achieve more in their life.

The path of least resistance for Steady Settlers is to follow conventional wisdom. They find comfort in following the straight path: in their mind, it's worked before, and it will work again. When they hold on to conventional wisdom, however, Steady Settlers continue to conform. They blend in with other Steady Settlers, and soon they lose their unique character. When Steady Settlers make a conscious choice to abandon conformity, they gain independence. Independence is the power and freedom to choose your own destiny. Steady Settlers have the tools inside to embark on an independent path, but they are too focused on staying put and among other like-minded settlers.

Finally, when Steady Settlers abandon their close-minded framework, they gain the power of adaptability. Steady Settlers miss out on opportunities to advance because their minds are closed to the world around them. When you open your mind, you leverage the power of adaptability to change your perspective and interact with the world around you.

Let's move on to the final Lemon Lifer, the Change Chaser.

Change Chaser

Give up	Gain
Appearances	Independence
Chasing	Introspection
Following	Individuality
Shortcuts	Tenacity
Instant gratification	Growth

Change Chasers work so hard to prop up appearances that they derive stature from others. However, when they give up their focus on appearances, they will gain independence. Change Chasers obviously have the independence switch inside them. After all, they're motivated to make a quick buck and will invest at least some time to change their life predicament. The issue is that all this chasing leaves little time for substantive self-introspection. Change Chasers need to assess their lives and reapply their ability to chase things to look inward.

Change Chasers get lost in the chase and expend much time and energy chasing and following others. When they give up following, they gain individuality. Change Chasers crave individuality, even if they follow others. When Change Chasers can express their individuality, they'll begin to lead lives with purpose.

Change Chasers love shortcuts. The fastest way from point A to point B means more money in their pocket. As a result, they're great at starting new tasks. They are also adept at quitting tasks when things get too hard. This start-and-stop way of life leaves lots of messes around, not to mention inconsistency. When Change Chasers give up shortcuts, they'll begin to build tenacity and learn that finishing tasks requires dedication, purpose, conviction, and direction.

Finally, Change Chasers want immediate change. They thrive on the art of the instant. However, true change takes time. Growth is a continual process, and their road to self-improvement comes when they reposition for a long-term trajectory.

To recap:

- Eternal Excusers *wait* for things to happen.
- Steady Settlers *watch* for things to happen.
- Change Chasers *hope* for things to happen.

In contrast, Daring Disruptors *make* things happen.

Once you know these four characters—the Eternal Excuser, Steady Settler, Change Chaser, and Daring Disruptor—and take a closer look at the people in your life, you will see these characters with increased clarity. You are surrounded by Lemon Lifers. They're everywhere. They outnumber Lemonade Lifers by a wide margin. Think about the people in your life—friends, family, acquaintances, colleagues, classmates, even strangers. Can you spot the Lemon Lifers? Here's one way to spot a Lemon Lifer without fail.

Some People Wait All Week for Friday

Lemon Lifers believe that success begets happiness; that is, when you become successful, you get happy.

However, psychologists and neuroscientists have shown empirically that the traditional model—that success leads to happiness—is broken. According to Shawn Achor, success doesn't lead to happiness; happiness drives success. It's what Achor calls the Happiness Advantage, which says that "happiness is the precursor to success, not merely the result." Per Achor, "the greatest competitive advantage in the modern economy is a positive and engaged brain." For example, he says that positivity at work leads to a 31 percent increase in productivity, 40 percent increased likelihood to get a promotion, 23 percent fewer stress-related symptoms, and 37 percent higher sales. Multiple research studies demonstrate that a positive effect makes us more engaged, energetic, creative, and motivated. Researchers Sonja Lyubomirsky, Laura King, and Ed Diener conducted a meta-analysis of 225 studies comprised of 275,000 total participants and found that happy people are successful in several areas of life, including career, income, friendship, marriage, and health.

Lemon Lifers follow conventional wisdom that says happiness is the result of success:

Work → Make money → Get happy

Eternal Excusers and Steady Settlers, in particular, often prioritize their jobs ahead of their families, friends, and hobbies. Why? So they can enjoy a happy retirement.

Finally, it's time. We get to be happy now.

Therefore, happiness comes—if it comes—at the end of their lives. Does that sound like a good deal to you? Retirement doesn't sound so golden when you say it like that.

Lemonade Lifers know that Lemon Lifers think about success and happiness upside down. Lemonade Lifers don't work to make money to get happy. They reject deferred happiness. They recognize up front that their golden years are not only in retirement. In the Lemonade Life, happiness starts today. There's no thirty-year waiting period.

Lemonade Lifers think life works like this:

Get happy → Access freedom → Achieve success

When you're happy today, you gain the power and freedom to achieve greatness in your life—however you define it. Happiness is the starting point for you to achieve greatness; being great is not what causes happiness. Freedom is more accessible because happiness fosters courage and confidence, which can empower you to make independent decisions.

Long-term happiness is not deferred happiness. Long-term happiness is making long-term, structural, and permanent changes to your habits and behaviors today to live the life you want.

These are simple, permanent changes. It's not feel happy today (short-term happiness) and feel bad tomorrow. It's not feel sad today (slog through the trenches now) to get happy tomorrow. It's make changes today, so you can feel happy today and happy tomorrow.

So, how do you "get happy"?

Five Simple Ways to Feel Happier Now

Want to know the secrets? Here are five easy ways to feel happier now:

Smile more.

We all know that we smile when we are happy. Therefore, it's common wisdom that happiness leads to smiling. But according to psychologists Tara Kraft and Sarah Pressman, smiling can also make you feel better and reduce stress. That flips conventional wisdom on its head, and suggests that smiling can lead to happiness. Their study in *Psychological Science* found that smiling can yield both psychological and physiological benefits.

Kraft and Pressman say that smiling can help you get through a stressful situation, even if the smile isn't genuine. And if you can make a genuine smile (known as a Duchenne smile, or "smiling with your eyes"), your heart rate may decrease during moments of stress.

That's not all. Psychoneuroimmunology research, which looks at the connection between your brain and immune system, has found that happiness can boost your body's immune system. Smiling also triggers a chemical reaction in your brain, which releases hormones such as dopamine, which can increase your feelings of happiness, and serotonin, the release of which can help reduce stress.

Be grateful.

What are the Seven Wonders of the World? Originally, they were the most impressive natural and man-made structures of the ancient world. To the ancient Greeks, the number seven represented the five planets known at the time, plus the sun and moon.

The Seven Wonders of the Ancient World were the following:

- Colossus of Rhodes
- Great Pyramid of Giza
- Hanging Gardens of Babylon
- Lighthouse of Alexandria
- Mausoleum at Halicarnassus
- Statue of Zeus at Olympia
- Temple of Artemis at Ephesus

Over the years, there have been other wonders of the world: the Empire State Building, the Taj Mahal, the Golden Gate Bridge, the Great Wall of

China, the Colosseum in Rome, the Hagia Sophia, Machu Picchu, Stonehenge, the Burj Khalifa, and many others.

What are *your* Seven Wonders of the World? They don't have to be physical structures or natural wonders you've seen on your travels.

Think about the seven things in your life that move you, that touch you, that inspire you. Think of the seven things that bring you hope and have changed the way you see the world.

It may be your children, your parents, your spouse. It may be a miracle in your life that you can't explain. It may be the things for which you're most grateful. Whatever you choose, these are the seven things that make your life complete.

The seven wonders are all about gratitude, which is strongly associated with more happiness. Gratitude is the antidote to entitlement. It's about being appreciative for what you have, where you came from, and your friends and family.

Buy experiences, not things.

What will you remember more—the last pair of shoes you bought, or the time you went dogsledding in Alaska?

Researchers at Cornell University and the University of California, San Francisco found that "experiential purchases" (which they define as "money spent on *doing*") provides more enduring happiness than "material purchases" (which they define as "money spent on *having*"). They also found that anticipation of the experiential purchase provides more happiness than waiting for a material possession.

Collect experiences that will stay with you a lifetime. Enjoy the anticipation and the experience. Build bonds with other people through shared adventures. Your experiences will inspire you, challenge you, move you.

You will gain more from the thrills and from the social interactions than any material asset can provide you.

Commit acts of kindness.

The next time you're in line at the grocery store, the movies, the drive-through, or anywhere else where you're buying something, pay for the person behind you.

Want to connect with someone instantly? Hold the door open for them and let them go first.

Want to make someone's day? Put money in their expired parking meter.

Want to lift someone's spirits? Make a care package and give it to someone in need.

These are only a few small acts of kindness that will brighten someone else's day. When you connect with people and touch their hearts, it not only strengthens humanity but also strengthens your soul.

Research from the University of Chicago and Northwestern University shows that when it comes to our happiness, the joy of giving outlasts the joy of receiving. Typically, happiness declines each time you experience the same event or activity, which psychologists call "hedonic adaptation." Studies show that giving something to others, rather than receiving the same thing, may be the exception to this principle.

In one experiment, researchers gave participants five dollars a day for five days. One group spent the money on themselves, while the second group spent it on others. All participants began the experiment with a similar happiness level. After five days, the first group experienced a self-reported decline in happiness each day, while the second group self-reported the same happiness level between days one and five. The results have several possible explanations, but one rationale, according to researchers, is that when people focus on themselves, they make social comparisons, which can make each experience less meaningful. In contrast, when people leave money in a tip jar or give to charity, they focus less on comparisons and more on the individual experience of giving, which creates happiness.

Empower other people.

Dolly Parton's father couldn't read or write. His circumstances required that he start working at a young age to help support his family. Although he was the smartest man she ever knew, she believed that his inability to read likely prevented him from reaching his dreams. Parton, who is a global country music icon and successful entrepreneur, didn't want to see others who couldn't read fail to realize their dreams. So she started the Imagination Library in honor of her father, Lee Parton, to champion childhood literacy.

The organization is a book-gifting program that mails high-quality books to children, regardless of income, from birth until they start school. The Imagination Library delivers more than one million books each month and has delivered over one hundred million books to children around the world.

The power to read is the power to dream, to expand your possibilities, and to access new opportunities. For Parton, that means her action will create a better life and future for millions of children.

When you lead like Dolly, you spread happiness, gain happiness, and empower others in immeasurable ways.

These five steps will spark the happiness that you then must nurture. We each have a different definition of happiness and fulfillment, so you'll need to identify the one that resonates most with you. Once you do, you don't need to wait—you can start living your happiness today.

Switch On: Perspective

Happiness, prosperity, and confidence all come from having the right perspective. If you see yourself in the descriptions of the Lemon Lifers in this book, consider it an opportunity to transform and adopt a new perspective. It's never too late. All it takes to begin your journey is an open mind and the courage to change. Eternal Excusers who stop making excuses should be welcomed. Steady Settlers who strive to become more independent should be encouraged. Change Chasers who are willing to commit for the long haul should be celebrated. Daring Disruptors are the ultimate exclusive club, but the path to membership is open to all. The power to change your life—no matter when you flip the perspective switch—lies only with you.

R IS FOR RISK

*Understand the rewards of risk
to make better decisions*

It's not because things are difficult that we dare not venture. It's because we dare not venture that they are difficult.

—Seneca

4

ESCAPE THE CHASM OF CAN'T

What Is the Chasm of Can't?

The Chasm of Can't is an environment where the people around you create barriers to your success and roadblocks to your achievements.

It happens in all aspects of our lives—with family, with friends, and at work. In the Chasm of Can't, the naysayers call the shots. They control the rules, limit your possibilities, and in some cases, define you. Boundaries are formed, progress is stalled, and outcomes are limited.

The Chasm of Can't is the driving force in the Lemon Life, and the primary reason why people make excuses, settle, chase change, and cannot make lemonade. They succumb to the fear of risk, and place other people's judgments above their own. Since they don't actively control their life path, they allow others to shape their destiny. Naturally, this interferes with their ability to realize their full potential.

No matter where you come from, how much money you have, or where you are in life, you've probably had someone tell you no.

"You can't go to this school because it's impossible to get in."

"You can't get that job because you're not qualified."

"You can't move there because you don't know anybody."

"You can't start that business because there's so much competition."

Have you heard this before? I have. How many times have you been told no? How many times has someone laughed at your dreams? How many times has someone doubted your abilities? How many times has someone not believed in you?

When we hear no, it can feel suffocating and limiting. When people tell you that you can't do something, their negativity often has nothing to do with you. Instead, others are projecting their own fears onto you.

They're afraid to apply because they don't want that rejection letter.

They're afraid to change jobs because they fear they won't get hired.

They're afraid to move because they don't know how they'll meet new people.

They're afraid to start a company because they don't know how to compete.

That someone could very well have been an Eternal Excuser. Eternal Excusers are everywhere: they are parents, teachers, bosses, friends, spouses, or family members.

Anyone can get trapped inside the Chasm of Can't, but Eternal Excusers are most susceptible. Ironically, the Chasm of Can't is their happy place. It's where they feel most comfortable. Inside the mind of every Eternal Excuser is a fence. A tall, fortified, electric fence that surrounds them in all directions. Someone *put* that fence there. So far, the Eternal Excuser hasn't tried to move it. Over time, the Eternal Excuser has learned not to climb, jump, or go anywhere near that fence. Why? Too much time. Too much effort.

The reality, however, is often far different from Eternal Excusers' perception. Up close, the fence is much smaller. It's not sturdy. Certainly not electric. If they would walk the perimeter, they would see the fence isn't even continuous. In other words, there are spots to break through to the other side. To their disadvantage, Eternal Excusers don't see the fence this way. Until they do—if they ever try—they're stuck. Stuck living inside a fence. This is their world, and many Eternal Excusers want you to live inside a fence too.

Don't let them push their insecurities onto you. Few things in life have strict prerequisites. Yes, if you can't throw a ninety-mile-an-hour fastball, you won't be a Major League Baseball pitcher. But there are no prerequisites to becoming a successful entrepreneur. The best ideas win, and you can have the best one. You don't have to go to business school to become a CEO. Likewise, you don't need political experience to win an election.

REMEMBER THIS: There will be people in your life who will root for you, support you, and love you.

And others won't get you. It's a fact of life. No matter what you do, how nice you are, how friendly you act, they won't be on your side. You can try hard and make the effort, but no matter what, they won't sing your praises. Maybe they're jealous. Maybe it's them. Maybe it's you.

Guess what?

It doesn't matter.

You'll reclaim so much time and energy in your life if you accept this truth. And when you live it every day, you're leading life on your own terms. You're not seeking approval or permission, or worrying what others think. You're focused on leading your best life—and it will feel great.

In contrast, when you allow the Chasm of Can't to dictate your path, you create self-imposed boundaries that will limit your life. Those limitations are like walking with sandbags tied to your ankles.

You can't run. You can't jump. You can't climb. We start to enter the danger zone when this outer dialogue (someone telling us no) becomes an inner monologue built on self-doubt ("well, maybe I can't"). When we begin to tell ourselves that we can't do it, or the odds are stacked against us, that's when we give in to the Chasm of Can't.

Let's put the Chasm of Can't in a financial context: "I can't live my dream life because I don't make enough money."

Now let's put the Chasm of Can't in a professional context: "I can't get that job because they'll never hire me."

Boundaries not only define us but also confine us, boxing us in.

Speaking of boxes, grab a piece of paper and pencil. Draw a two-inch-by-two-inch box, and make sure the box's borders are thick.

Inside that box, write all your life goals: what you want to achieve personally, professionally, financially, and spiritually.

How was it, trying to fit all your life goals into that box?

The problem is, you can't. The box is too confining. The box's borders represent all the boundaries in your life. Those are the same fences that Eternal Excusers live inside of every day. When we set boundaries around our life

45

goals, we set automatic limitations on achievements. There is no room for goals because the thick borders overpower them.

Now, erase the box. As you erase, think about the roadblocks that you're clearing in your own life. Erase what has been holding you back, what's been challenging in your life. As you wipe your paper, think about what you're washing away. You're washing away your barriers. You're creating a clean slate to achieve your goals. It's much easier now. There's more room. There's more freedom to write, to think, to visualize. When the borders disappear, there's no longer a physical box—there's just free space and open pastures. Throughout your life, I want you to keep coming back to this theme: clear the roadblocks that inhibit your progress.

How do you remove these roadblocks? You reposition through three strategies:

1. Check Your Wolfpack
2. Write the Millionaire's Check
3. Learn the Inventor's Secret

The first way to escape the Chasm of Can't is to check your wolfpack.

Check Your Wolfpack

Your wolfpack is composed of your inner circle, the people to whom you give your time, energy, and attention. Your wolfpack can be your friends, family, coworkers, or anyone else who plays a central role in your life. Author Jim Rohn said that you're the average of the five people with whom you associate most. Rohn's observation is related, at least partly, to the law of averages, which says that the result will be the average of all outcomes. Therefore, think of your wolfpack as your most important group of influencers, who can impact your perspectives, your behaviors, your mood, and even your health. A metastudy of more than three hundred thousand adults across all ages showed that having the right wolfpack can increase your longevity by 50 percent. Research also has shown that having the wrong wolfpack can increase risk of heart problems, high blood pressure, and obesity.

When was the last time you took a hard look at your most influential group?

Who's in your wolfpack? Name them out loud.

Think about the names on your list. Are the people on that list the people you really want around you? Ask yourself: Does my wolfpack lift me up or tear me down? More important, are you a better person from spending your time and energy with each person in your wolfpack? Are they helping you achieve your dreams, or are they blocking your path?

If one or more people are tearing you down, it's time for them to leave your wolfpack. More specifically, it's time for you to remove them from your wolfpack. You don't have room in your life for unnecessary baggage. You want assets, not liabilities.

Spend time with the people you admire, who mentor and counsel you, who challenge you, and who make you your best self. If you want to work in marketing, spend time with natural storytellers who understand people, products, and markets. If you want to learn more about music, spend time with composers, performers, and producers who can share their creativity with you. If you want to work in medicine, spend time with physicians, nurses, and first responders to understand problem-solving and decision-making.

Wolfpacks aren't a one-way interaction, but a symbiotic relationship. For every person who helps, teaches, and changes you, be sure to pay it forward and help others realize their dreams.

Eternal Excusers don't curate their wolfpack. Instead, they find like-minded Eternal Excusers with whom they can commiserate. However, Daring Disruptors understand the power of curation—the ability to pick and choose who stays in your inner circle and who you depend on to lift you up.

Curating your wolfpack—and how you spend your time—takes little effort, but will have an enormous impact on your life. When you have the right wolfpack, it's easier to escape the Chasm of Can't. Your wolfpack is there to support and lift you, not block or limit you.

Even so, your wolfpack can't do the work for you. Your wolfpack can mentor, consult, counsel, and encourage you to dare and disrupt. They can provide the positive energy necessary for achievement, but you're the one who must scale the fence. The boundaries set by others are just that: boundaries set by others. You don't have to accept them. Only you are responsible for your own limitations.

Now, create a second wolfpack. Unlike your first wolfpack, your second wolfpack is composed of people you don't know but wish you did. Think of this wolfpack as your all-star team of history's greatest. If you could assemble your starting five, who would you pick and why? These are people you look up to and to whom you can listen. Ask yourself: What would Nelson Mandela do in this situation? How would Elizabeth Cady Stanton confront the naysayers? How would Martin Luther King Jr. inspire you to have an impact? The diversity of ideas, skills, and talents in your dream team wolfpack will expand your reach and provide greater depth in your tool set, to tackle even the greatest challenges.

So now you have two wolfpacks: your everyday, go-to friends and mentors, and the trailblazers who have come before you and whom you aspire to become.

THE 5X RULE. The 5X Rule is a simple tool to quickly identify, assess, and curate the key aspects of your life. You don't need to stop with your wolfpack. Let's take this "law of five" a step further to see how the 5X Rule works in practice.

On a piece of paper, draw five large boxes. In each box, list five items.

- Box 1: List the five members of your wolfpack.
- Box 2: List the five people with whom you spend the most time at work.
- Box 3: List the five activities you do most often.
- Box 4: List the five times in the past year when you were truly happy.
- Box 5: List the five times in the past year when you risked something.

Look at your responses. The 5X Rule helps you answer this essential question: Is this who you want to be? Do these lists, when viewed together, reflect the best you? If not, it's time to update how you choose to spend your time, energy, and focus. You can use the 5X Rule to analyze any part of your life. Like your wolfpack, these lists aren't permanent. Change them to the life you want to lead, not the life you're living.

When you replace boundaries with possibilities, you open your pathway and redefine a life without limit. Those possibilities are best defined in the Millionaire's Check.

Write the Millionaire's Check: What You and Jim Carrey Are About to Have in Common

Your mind-set positions you to expand your possibilities. Your commitment and drive propel you to reach goals. Too many people want to focus first on action because they think action is what gets the job done. That's true, but before you act, you need the right foundation. You can be the most execution-oriented person in the world, but if you're operating with a faulty mind-set, you'll never get off the ground. Get the mind-set right first, and everything else flows from there.

Daring Disruptors reach their potential because each breath begins with what they can do, not with what they can't. They remove roadblocks and create opportunities to lead the lives they want. They're unafraid to dream big, beyond the fence. Those big dreams begin with the Millionaire's Check.

Grab a checkbook and tear off the first check. Make out the check to yourself . . . for $10 million.

Yes, $10 million.

Don't worry—this won't cost a thing. Keep that check in a safe place, where you can look at it every single day. This check should be your reminder of the possibility in your life, a symbol for what your life can become.

When Jim Carrey first tried to make it in Hollywood, it wasn't smooth sailing. He had little money, and the acting roles he craved remained elusive. Carrey used to park on Mulholland Drive in Los Angeles every night and give himself a pep talk. As he told Oprah Winfrey years later, he used to convince himself that directors loved him, people he admired respected him, and he was going to be famous. Carrey used the power of visualization to remind himself of his innate ability to make people laugh. And he would leave each night feeling better—and with power to charge forward the next day.

"Well, I do have these [roles]," he would tell himself, as he later said to Oprah. "They are out there. I just don't have a hold of them yet."

At one point, Carrey decided to write himself a check for $10 million for "acting services rendered" and postdated it Thanksgiving 1995. He kept the check in his wallet. Over the next few years, Carrey began to build his career in Hollywood and hone his comedic craft. With each television and film project, he referred to the check in his wallet and never lost sight of that goal.

Following his box office success in *Ace Ventura: Pet Detective*, *The Mask*, and *Dumb and Dumber*, Carrey surpassed his goal when he reportedly received a $20 million advance for the 1996 film *The Cable Guy*.

Be like Jim Carrey: leverage the power of visualization. Use the check you just wrote to remind you of what's possible in life. Importantly, the check represents the bold goals that many people dream of, but don't want to do the work to reach. Your goal doesn't have to be money, by the way. For many people, it's not. So find the "check" that works best for you.

It's up to you, and only you, to choose whether the Chasm of Can't thrives in your life. Carrey made the choice for himself, not the casting agents and directors who turned him down. It all starts when you allow yourself to commit to a goal greater than your circumstances. It continues when that goal is central to your life. It flourishes when you remind yourself daily that what seems impossible to others truly is possible.

Lemon Lifers don't understand this. But now you do.

Learn the Inventor's Secret

Someone else who also understands the power of creating possibility in life is an inventor. Inventors live only in a world of possibility—their art is to redefine what is possible. Their ability to think unconventionally and without limitation enables them to disrupt and change the landscape. You can learn a lot by studying inventors.

I want you to meet two of them, who will forever change the way you approach life. They both thrived due to the Inventor's Secret.

I'm about to tell you one of the number one things you can do to ensure success in your life. But it's probably not what you think.

It's your willingness to fail.

That sounds strange because not many people are willing to fail. After all, winning has been ingrained into our psyche. There are winners and losers. The choice has always been binary. And everyone wants to be a winner. From a young age, we want to win the soccer game or win the argument with our siblings. At work, we want to win the sales pitch and beat the competition. Inherently, we want things to go right. It's human inclination to shun failure. No one likes to lose. Failure is associated with disappointment, humiliation, and ridicule. At the same time, because of these fears, we prevent ourselves from taking leaps that we otherwise could take, if we shifted our perspective and understanding of what it means to fail.

This is what inventors understand, but many others don't.

Another way you escape from the Chasm of Can't is not to run from failure, but to embrace it. That sounds counterintuitive. If the goal is always to win, why should you embrace failure? Fundamentally, the Lemonade Life is about winning. Winning is always the first and best option. But we don't need to hide from or be ashamed of failure. If you're willing to win, you should be willing to lose. You should be willing to be bold and take actions at which you may fail before you win. Why?

We lose when we don't aspire to take chances to win. We lose when we don't reach beyond our comfort zone for a chance to be better. We lose when we don't take risks to reach for greatness. The failure isn't in failing—it's in failing to dare, aspire, act, and progress. It's counterintuitive to think of failure as your friend, because failure means you didn't win. You lost, right? It didn't work out. You screwed up. That's the commonly held view of failure. That's also how failure looks in the Lemon Life. Just ask an Eternal Excuser.

Eternal Excusers give up before they even take the plunge. They've already predicted the outcome. They lose the race before the pistol has been fired. Like Steady Settlers, Eternal Excusers are afraid of failure because of how they will be perceived. So they don't embrace risks or step outside their comfort zones, for fear of ridicule or judgment.

Now, let's look at failure in the Lemonade Life. Through the eyes of the Daring Disruptor, failure isn't a dead end, but a pathway. Daring Disruptors take leaps for themselves, not to impress others. Over time, that independent mind-set *increases* their reputational capital. Why? Daring Disruptors are willing to put themselves out there and make things happen. They're willing to take the hits, get scraped, and get bruised. Daring Disruptors also fear failure. After all, they're not superhuman. It's okay to be afraid of the unknown. Here's the difference: For Daring Disruptors, fear of failure isn't a deterrent to disruption or a roadblock to action. Daring Disruptors recognize that it's okay to fail.

Failure is about taking the initial risk outside your comfort zone, even if the outcome isn't what you desired. If you're a Daring Disruptor, failure isn't extending its hand to push you down. Failure is lending a hand to lift you up. It's okay to fail on your quest to succeed. More important, though, is how you respond to failure. Despite common wisdom, failure isn't the antithesis of success. Rather, failure is about learning and experimentation.

Ask James Dyson.

This Inventor Failed Five Thousand Times
Just to Make a Better Vacuum

James Dyson spent fifteen years and created 5,126 prototypes before he invented his bestselling bagless, dual-cycle vacuum.

At the time, the idea of a bagless vacuum cleaner was foreign. How could a vacuum cleaner without a bag collect all that debris? Where would it all go? Imagine all the Eternal Excusers who laughed at Dyson's idea. At that time, vacuums had bags. Those boundaries were set by others. Dyson wasn't trying to make a better vacuum. He sought to change the vacuum as we knew it. He focused on the possibilities, not the boundaries.

Daring Disruptors drive innovation, spur technological growth, and create breakthroughs that redefine how we live. When inventors like Dyson dream big, they're often dreaming bigger than other dreamers. This doesn't mean the biggest dreams win. It means that they have a vision for how it can be, rather than how it is.

Often, with big dreams comes a long road to realization. That process likely will be met with trial and error, twists and turns, and outright failure. As an inventor like Dyson knows, failure is an iterative process. Failure should propel you to take the next step and do it better—and do it differently. Daring Disruptors understand that failure leads somewhere. Success rarely is immediate or seamless. If it is, then you're not setting big enough goals.

As an inventor, Dyson spent a lifetime failing. We know him now as a knighted billionaire, and we admire his creative prowess and track record of success. But his *failures* got him there. So Daring Disruptors can often fail more than they succeed. Like Dyson, sometimes doing things the wrong way helps you discover something that other people haven't. Only then can you test, challenge, and question why something fails. The "why" leads you to the solution. Often, failure isn't the deterrent to new opportunities, but is a potential springboard to something better. Those who aren't afraid to jump in and get dirty will have an upper hand.

There may be times when you do everything you think you're supposed to do, but fail anyway. Unlike Eternal Excusers, Daring Disruptors don't worry whether life is unfair. If things don't work out "as expected," the way Daring Disruptors respond to failure sets them apart.

This Future Billionaire Lost Everything

At age twenty-seven, Sam Walton opened his first Ben Franklin variety store in Newport, Arkansas. In five years, Walton more than tripled the store's annual revenue from $72,000 to $250,000. However, when Walton tried to renew his lease, the unexpected happened.

Walton learned that his lease didn't have a renewal clause, a detail he had overlooked. Despite Walton's success, his landlord, P. K. Holmes, refused to renew his lease. Holmes, the local department store owner, figured that his son could operate the successful variety store instead. Walton had no alternative in Newport to relocate his store, and Holmes knew it. So Holmes forced Walton to sell him the business. Walton thought he'd built the best store in the region and had done everything right.

Now, he'd lost it all.

What would you do if you were Walton? Many people in his position would take another job or open a new kind of business in Newport.

What did Walton do?

He reinvented himself. He opened a self-service variety store about 275 miles away in Bentonville, Arkansas, and over time, he became the largest independent variety store operator in the United States. How did he do it? He was proactive and took an unconventional approach.

Unlike most retail chains, Walton focused on smaller towns, which were located closer to the company's regional warehouses. He instituted a new self-service model, which caused shoppers to spend more money. As Richard Tedlow notes in *Giants of Enterprise*, Walton purchased merchandise in large volumes to offer lower prices and opted for a single cashier, to reduce payroll costs. With these changes, Walton could pass on more savings to consumers, which helped grow his business. Sometimes, your lowest point can be your highest one.

These principles became the backbone for his next act. At age forty-four, in search of a new idea with higher volume and revenue, Walton started a venture that he called Walmart—and it made him a billionaire.

How did Walton bounce back from failure? He had signed a bad contract, lost his business, and been forced to leave town. Well, the situation was more than getting back up and fighting another day. Daring Disruptors like Walton understand that dwelling on past mistakes is fruitless and will only compound failure into a lingering roadblock.

Daring Disruptors tackle problems head-on and don't let others define them. Holmes may have put Walton out of business in Newport, but Walton knew that temporary roadblocks can be overcome, and circumstances can be changed. Daring Disruptors also know how to reinvent. Walton had the foresight to rebuild his business in an unconventional location, and to think critically about logistics, merchandising, and inventory. He relied on his intuition to build one of the world's greatest retail empires.

Nineteen years after Walton left town, he returned to Newport when Walmart Store #18 opened there. Soon, customers in Newport chose Walmart, and Walton's old Ben Franklin store, which was still operated by the landlord's son, was forced to shut down.

Accepting failure doesn't mean giving in to failure. Dyson and Walton showed us how Daring Disruptors make failure temporary. It happened. It's done. The way you reposition determines your next chapter.

5

EMBRACE THE REWARDS OF RISK

Imagine that there's a plate of warm, homemade, fresh-baked chocolate chip cookies with your name on it.

To retrieve this free, delicious prize, all you have to do is walk ten minutes up a steep hill.

Would you do it?

As you ponder that question, Lemon Lifers already know the answer.

Once Change Chasers hear the words "chocolate chip cookies," they're in.

Once Eternal Excusers hear the words "steep hill," they're out.

That's because Lemon Lifers make decisions based on risk *or* reward.

There's either a great reward ("Who doesn't love chocolate chip cookies?"), so they pursue the opportunity, or there's too much risk ("A hill? Are you kidding me?"), so they avoid it.

Change Chasers focus mostly on the rewards, so they often miss the risks.

Eternal Excusers focus mostly on the risks, so they often miss the rewards.

In contrast, Daring Disruptors approach risks and rewards in three primary ways:

1. They use the risk-reward ratio.
2. They protect the downside.
3. They embrace the rewards of risk.

To assess risk and reward, Daring Disruptors also seek more information up front—such as how steep the hill is, how long the hike is, and how many cookies there are.

Use the Risk-Reward Ratio

Daring Disruptors don't make decisions through the lens of risk or reward. Rather, they focus on the relationship between risk *and* reward, which is key to better decision-making.

Notice the differences among Eternal Excusers, Change Chasers, and Daring Disruptors when evaluating an investment opportunity:

- Eternal Excusers say, "Oh, I don't invest. You can't make any money." *They undervalue the reward and overvalue the risk.*
- Change Chasers say, "This biotech stock can increase 50 percent in two months. It's a no-brainer." *They overvalue the reward and undervalue the risk.*
- Daring Disruptors say, "This stock could triple by year-end, but it also might decline 25 percent." *When you understand the potential for upside and downside, you can make a more informed decision.*

To make better decisions, Daring Disruptors use a tool called the risk-reward ratio—or reward-risk ratio, if you list the reward first—which is the amount of risk you're willing to take relative to the potential reward you can earn. In a risk-reward ratio, risk and reward are inextricably linked. Importantly, this isn't a pessimistic or risk-averse approach. Rather, it's about understanding the total implications of any decision, so you make fully informed choices that lead to better outcomes.

How do you use the risk-reward ratio to make better decisions? A risk-reward ratio says that for every opportunity where you could lose, your potential reward should be some multiple of that potential loss. Traditionally, the risk-reward ratio is used in a financial context, where you can evaluate the merits of a financial decision by quantifying the upside (how much you might gain) and downside (how much you might lose) potential of the underlying opportunity. However, you can also use the risk-reward ratio in other contexts. For example, here's a quick way to evaluate a new job offer by applying the risk-reward ratio. Start by creating a traditional plus-minus inventory, where you list all the positive and negative attributes of the prospective job, and then score each attribute from 1–5, with 5 being the highest and 1 being the lowest.

Your list might look something like this:

Should I Accept This Job?

Positive	Score	Negative	Score
Salary	5	Work-Life Balance	3
Benefits	4	Commute	3
Culture	5		
Team	4		
Total	18	Total	6

The sum of the positive attributes, or rewards, of the job is eighteen. The sum of the negative attributes, or risks, is six. That makes a reward-risk ratio of 18:6. When you divide eighteen by six, the reward-risk ratio is reduced to 3:1. A good rule of thumb is to pursue opportunities where you think you have at least a 3:1 reward-risk ratio. This means that your potential "win" (reward) should be three times the amount of your potential "loss" (risk). Since your own risk tolerance is unique, you may want a higher reward-risk ratio, to provide more comfort. For a 5:1 reward-risk ratio, for example, your potential win should be at least five times your potential loss. No matter the reward-risk ratio that you determine, it's only one data point in your overall evaluation, and it's always an educated guess, not an exact science.

When you evaluate a decision, approach the upside and downside with equal consideration. Here's how too many people think about decisions: "I want to go to Hollywood and be a movie star, like Leonardo DiCaprio or Scarlett Johansson. I just need that big break, and I'll be set for life. If it doesn't work, then at least I lived my life with no regrets."

No. That isn't the way to make decisions.

You haven't thought about the risk-reward. You got the reward part right—that's easy. Everyone understands the upside: you're rich and famous. What about the downside? What are you fundamentally giving up by making that decision? It's good to live with no regrets, it's good to take chances, and it's good to be unafraid to accomplish things. However, you're potentially forfeiting years of your life, time with your family, and lack of a steady income stream.

Is that a bet you're willing to take? For some people, the answer is yes. For others, it's not worth the risk, despite the potential reward.

If you're going to weigh benefits and risks, do it in a balanced and authentic way, so you can make a more informed decision. That means quantifying the downside in the same manner you quantify the upside. Otherwise, you're tricking yourself into believing you understand risk-reward, but you only understand reward. It's always easier to think about the upside; that's where optimists gravitate. However, you're creating a biased choice. It's an easy way to convince yourself that you're making a real decision, but it's an unfair comparison.

One strategy to bring more clarity to your decision-making approach is to jump to the future and look backward. Imagine that you try to be an actor, and you spend thirty years auditioning, but you don't get your big break. How would you feel? When you're fifty years old and you haven't gotten hired in a lead role, will the struggle have been worth it? You may have more clarity if you think about your career at the end, looking back.

Whether you're evaluating an investment or choosing your next job, your mastery of the risk-reward ratio will help lead you to a better outcome.

Protect the Downside

It's human nature to focus on how much money you can make. However, you should be focusing on how much money you can *lose* as a relationship to how much money you can make. One of the most important rules of decision-making is to protect the downside, which means to mitigate your risk. But too many people let their excitement about an opportunity subjectively cloud their judgment regarding the true downside risk.

Remember, risk-reward has two components: upside (reward) and downside (risk). Focusing on the upside is the easy part, but what matters—the downside—is often considered secondarily. Why? The downside is the part of the bet that can hurt your reward. When you control or limit the downside, you help protect the fruits of your labor.

So, how do you protect your downside? Here are three simple, actionable ways that anyone can mitigate risk:

- Make your money on the buy.
- Control your position sizes.
- Know when to quit.

Make your money on the buy.

Most people think they make their money when they *sell*. That's when they cash out and count their profit.

But your money is made on the *buy*. It's about the legwork you do before you make the commitment. For example, think about buying a home. If you know the structural condition of the home, safety of the neighborhood, and quality of the schools before you commit to buy the home, then you'll understand more than most "buyers" ever will. It's easier to say no before you've committed than after you're fully on board. You can never have perfect information or predict every risk, but you can do your homework, conduct your due diligence, and understand what you're "buying." Then, when the risks appear, you'll be more prepared.

Focusing on your entry point may seem like short-term thinking. On the contrary, you're investing up front to have a more successful exit. It's short-term attention to protect your long-term trajectory. No matter the decision in your life, your exit is never your defining moment. Make your money on the buy.

Control your position sizes.

Position sizing is about rank-ordering what's most important to you, then directing more time and energy toward those efforts.

In investing, you control your position sizes by putting more money in your highest conviction investments (where you have the most confidence) and relatively less money in your lowest conviction investments (where you have the least confidence). You develop confidence in your decisions by doing the work up front. If you're right on your bigger bets, they drive your investment performance, and if you're wrong on your smaller bets, they have relatively less impact. Could the reverse happen, and you're wrong on your bigger bets and right on your smaller bets? Yes, but the point is that you mitigated risk by investing in your highest-conviction ideas, so the chances of the reverse outcome are lower. Daring Disruptors invest more in what they know and less in what they don't. Contrast this strategy with Change Chasers who, in the name of speculation, invest in everything. Controlling your position size is different from diversification, which says to spread your money in different types of investments, so you don't have all your eggs in one basket.

In life, you can control your position sizes by spending more time with people who uplift you and more effort on opportunities that inspire you. Focus on the people and opportunities that yield the biggest benefits, whether personally, professionally, financially, emotionally, or however you categorize them. Likewise, dedicate less time and effort to people and opportunities that demotivate you. It sounds simple in principle, but how often do you practice this in a systematic way?

You can make those judgments only after you put in the work to get informed about your choices. Since you're rank-ordering your time and effort, you don't have to make all the right decisions. No decision is a sure bet, no matter how much you prepare. The goal is to do your homework up front and then dedicate more time and effort to the people and opportunities you're most confident will add value to your life, thereby increasing your chances of success and minimizing your risks of failure. When you rank these decisions and focus more time and effort on those where you have the highest conviction, you'll be more organized and more in control of your destiny.

Know when to quit.

We are taught to never quit, to see things through, and to never give up.

However, giving up and knowing when to fold aren't the same thing. The fastest way to keep losing is to hold on to a loser. It can be the stressful job that's leading nowhere. It can be the relationship that should've ended years earlier. It can be the member of your wolfpack who isn't uplifting you. But we don't want to give up. So we endure, we hang on, and we accept. That's what we're taught to do. We're afraid of failure, afraid what others will think, and afraid of being labeled a quitter. Instead of focusing on our own happiness, we focus on the potential backlash. We carry the burden, we support the bad habit, and we relight the flame, even if we should blow out the candle.

"Oh, it's a temporary setback."

"Things will improve."

"It's not their fault."

However, the loser you're holding on to may not recover. It takes discipline to escape a losing situation, particularly when you've invested time, energy, or money. Knowing when to quit is one of the best ways to help you protect, and maximize, your upside. While sooner is often better, it's never too late to reposition your compass before experiencing further downside.

Embrace the Rewards of Risk

Protecting your downside is half the puzzle. The other half is about finding the right risks to take. Where should you look for opportunities?

Be Like the Guy Who Invented the Lollipop Stick Machine

It's easy to run to Silicon Valley or Wall Street for opportunities, because they're centers of wealth and power. It's easy to choose a tech startup because it can make you rich. In contrast, going a different direction from the majority can look odd and make you stand out. Some people might shake their heads, thinking you're a fool who has wasted an opportunity.

News flash: You don't have to create a tech company or hedge fund to make it big. You don't have to be Thomas Edison or Albert Einstein to create impact. To strike it rich during the California gold rush, you didn't have to be a miner. They could've opened hotels (miners needed shelter), started restaurants (miners needed food), or sold tools (miners needed supplies).

Almost everyone knows who Bill Gates, Jeff Bezos, and Steve Jobs are. They're household names today, but only because they did something that no one else was doing already. The risks they took created the industries that so many want to be a part of today. When they started, however, their classmates weren't all flocking to Palo Alto or Seattle. Remember that truth when you create your next opportunity; these next inventors did. You've likely never heard their names, but you've used their inventions.

Ernie Fraze: Inventor of the Pop-Top Aluminum Can

It's one of the most recognizable and refreshing sounds in the world, and it's all because of Ernie Fraze. While at a picnic in 1959, Fraze, an engineer, realized that he forgot his can opener for the drinks. Yes, drinks used to be opened with can openers or even keys, because you needed a tool to open your can. His solution that day? Like many endeavoring hackers, he found an alternative can opener: a car bumper.

Months later, during a restless night's sleep, he thought more about the can-opener dilemma. Others had conceived of a pop-top before, but the tops often malfunctioned. Fraze realized that the secret was in strengthening the rivet in the can. When the pop-top was attached to the prescored rivet located in the center of the can, the lever could be pulled without snapping.

Fraze sold the invention to Alcoa and later built a can-end machinery supplier that generated more than $500 million in annual revenue.

LESSON: Look for opportunities to be daring in everyday life. If other experts already have tried and failed, thank them for helping you determine what doesn't work, so you can focus on what does.

Sam Born: Inventor of the Automatic Lollipop Stick Machine

While he didn't invent the lollipop or the lollipop stick, Sam Born, a Russian immigrant, saw an opportunity to create more efficiency in the manufacturing process. In 1912, Born invented the eponymous Born Sucker Machine, which mechanically inserts a stick into a lollipop.

Born started Just Born, a family-owned candy manufacturer that makes recognizable candy brands such as Peeps, Mike and Ike, and Hot Tamales. For his lollipop stick machine, Born was awarded the key to the city of San Francisco in 1916.

LESSON: You can find a better, faster, and easier way to create efficiencies. That's what Daring Disruptors do.

Hymen Lipman: Inventor of the Modern Pencil Eraser

In the 1850s, there were pencils, and there were erasers. However, there were no pencils with erasers. Hymen Lipman, a stationer, changed that in 1858 when he registered the first patent for a pencil with an attached eraser. He sold the patent to Joseph Reckendorfer for $100,000.

In 1875, the US Supreme Court ruled in *Reckendorfer v. Faber* that the pencil-eraser combination was not a legitimate invention. In delivering the opinion of the Court, Justice Ward Hunt wrote, "The combination, to be patentable, must produce a different force or effect or result in the combined forces or processes from that given by their separate parts. There must be a new result produced by their union; if not so, it is only an aggregation of separate elements." As a result, pencil manufacturers such as A. W. Faber could sell pencil-eraser combinations without compensating Reckendorfer.

LESSON: Here, two entrepreneurs played the game. One won. One lost. But both dared.

Charles Brannock: Inventor of the *Brannock Device to Measure Shoe Size*

In 1925, Charles F. Brannock, the son of a shoe entrepreneur, invented the Brannock Device to measure length, width, and arch of a foot to determine the right shoe size. Brannock, who attended Syracuse University, spent two years developing his invention, which became the standard shoe measurement device in the United States for nearly a century.

Before Brannock's invention, customers settled for a wooden block for shoe measurements. Brannock's device did wonders for his father's shoe store, Park-Brannock Shoe Co., in Syracuse.

During World War II, the US Army hired Brannock to ensure its boots and shoes were sized properly.

LESSON: When there is an opportunity to do something better, do it. When the old way of doing things is imprecise, introduce precision.

Bette Nesmith Graham: Inventor of Liquid Paper to Correct Typos

Bette Nesmith Graham, a high school dropout, was an executive secretary to the chairman of the board of Texas Bank and Trust. With the advent of electric typewriters, Nesmith and her fellow secretaries increasingly made typos while learning to use the new machines. An artist in her spare time, Nesmith knew that painters simply painted over their mistakes. Why not do the same with typos?

In 1956, Nesmith created her own "Mistake Out" concoction of white tempera-based paint, which she mixed in her kitchen blender with dye, to match her company's stationery. With a small brush, she covered each typo on paper to hide her mistakes. When she started spending more time on her side hustle, including handing out samples to other secretaries at work, her boss unexpectedly fired her.

Undeterred, Nesmith's small side hustle became her full-time endeavor. Later, she changed the name of her product to Liquid Paper. Over the next twenty years, Nesmith went from selling one hundred bottles per month to selling the company to Gillette for $47.5 million.

LESSON: Losing your job may be the best thing that happens to you.

To make an impact, you don't have to become a household name. Remember—be like the guy who invented the lollipop stick machine.

Here's another secret: you don't have to earn unlimited money to find fulfillment. Becoming a billionaire doesn't have to be the benchmark. Our society places a huge premium on wealth. For many people, the rewards of life have become a state of financial happiness. But your life doesn't need to be defined by money alone. The billionaire benchmark doesn't have to be your benchmark. Many paths allow you to create impact and find fulfillment that meets your own definition of success.

Don't live other people's version of happiness. The risks you take are uniquely yours, and therefore, the rewards you enjoy should be the same. Leading the Lemonade Life is about your happiness, not theirs. Most people already know what makes them happy on the inside. They just ignore it.

Fulfillment comes from your efforts, ideas, and actions. You're recognized for what you created and how you changed others' lives.

You can create impact in many ways that are unrelated to financial gain. The magnitude of your impact is less important than whether you are creating impact. You can cure a life-threatening disease, or you can save the life of one patient. You can develop a new teaching method that helps millions of students learn more easily, or you could touch the life of one student who will be forever inspired. You could invent the next technology to simplify the lives of a billion people, or you can help ten people learn to use the internet. Find your niche. Look where others don't. Focus on creating impact. That's how you embrace risk.

But what do you do when the risks you take don't yield the benefits you desire? Translation: What happens when you fail? Failure can offer more to your life than you realize. We've all heard that it's okay to fail because doing so is part of life, but that is harder to accept in practice. However, failure isn't a dark cloud that we must force ourselves to welcome and accept. If you ask a Daring Disruptor, they'll tell you they treat failure not as an enemy, but as a friend.

Five Reasons Why Failure Can Be Your Friend

There are many reasons why we don't often take risks. We don't believe the result will be worth our time, effort, or money. We don't think the return is worth the risk. The most striking reason is that we often associate risk with failure. Failure can have lasting consequences—not only financial, but also emotional or mental. Failure hurts. However, failure also toughens you and provides a wealth of free information and feedback that will benefit you as much, if not more, than any success. Success helps remind you of your greatness. Failure reminds you of what's possible when you succeed.

REMEMBER THIS: Everyone gets a shot at redemption. It's what you do with failure that defines you.

Here are five reasons why failure can be your friend. As we learned with the Inventor's Secret, this is how Daring Disruptors think about failure, and how you should too.

Failure Provides Clarity

Use failure to study why you failed, and to learn about yourself in ways you can't when you always succeed. When you succeed, how often do you sit back and examine why? Almost never, because when we win, we're happy and satisfied. This is how Steady Settlers live. But this can lead to less introspection, because whatever you did worked. When you fail, it's often easier to see why. Maybe you didn't try hard enough, didn't practice hard enough, didn't have a competitive game plan, or just had a bad day. You can assess what went wrong, diagnosing the root causes of your preparation, actions, performance, missteps, and outcomes. It's not about self-blame. It's about undoing the bad habits, the wrong choices, or the uninformed strategy.

Confront your failures. Don't run from them. Don't wallow in them. Study them. Learn from them. Understand what went wrong, why you think it went wrong, and how it went wrong.

REMEMBER THIS: You may feel defeated when you undergo this introspective process, but you've received priceless data that you can use to reprogram yourself for the next fight.

Failure Helps You Take New Risks

When you fail, you learn, grow, show courage, and take risks. If you always succeed, you're doing something wrong. You're not being daring or bold or taking chances. Instead, you're being a Steady Settler—going through life playing it safe.

Why? It feels better to avoid failure because failure is a confirmation of limitation. You need to fall, get bruised, take some hits. Get in the arena. It's okay to get dirty.

REMEMBER THIS: There's no shame in failing. You must take that first step. You must commit to try. The more you try, the more opportunities you create.

Failure Provides a Springboard to New Beginnings

We think that when we fail, life is over. This is the end. We lost the game. We didn't win the business. We blew the sales pitch. We didn't get promoted. We blew our investment.

Not so.

At the time, these are unhappy moments. No one cheers when you lose. The natural reaction to failure may include shame, defeat, and embarrassment.

But failure also can be a window to new beginnings. If you identify the why behind the failure, it can be a launchpad to rehabilitate yourself. It's never the last contest. You'll live another day, and next time you'll be better prepared. Think of your previous failure as the practice round. You tested the waters and got to see what worked and what didn't.

REMEMBER THIS: Failure is free feedback about what to do better next time.

Failure Humbles You

If you always win, you get complacent. Why would you ever try new things or take on new challenges, if whatever you do right now works? After a while, you not only become complacent, but you also become afraid to fail or do anything that jeopardizes your current state. When you don't expand your reach or challenge your way of life, you get lazy. You get stuck in life's daily routines. Those days soon turn to months and years. You live the Lemon Life.

In the Lemonade Life, you view the world more clearly when you see a top and a bottom. If you're always sitting in your comfort zone, you don't think about falling. And if you don't think about falling, then you're certainly not thinking about life at the bottom.

Too many would rather be at the top; they think life is easier there. The problem with being at the top is twofold. First, when you're always at the top, you can lose sight of reality and may lose your edge. Second, when you're at the top, you can either maintain your position, or you can go down. But when you're at the bottom, you can see the entire spectrum. The only way to look is up.

REMEMBER THIS: At the bottom, it can stay bad, but it can't get much worse. Lift your head. You'll see that it's all upside from here.

Failure Is Less Scary the More You Fail

Often, the fear of failure is worse than failure itself.

When you're fearful, you miss opportunities. Eternal Excusers and Steady

Settlers fall into this category. Their conscious or unconscious calculation is that seizing the opportunity is outweighed by the risk of trying. Therefore, they choose inaction over action, and claim defeat before they step on the field.

You may fail the first time. But learning to cope with failure will make you less fearful the next time. You may fail again, but you'll be less fearful after the second try than you were before the first. Failure can extend its hand to help you along the path. Get back up if you get knocked down and reach for that open hand.

REMEMBER THIS: Once you're in the arena, the unknown doesn't feel as unknown. It's more familiar after putting yourself out there.

The more often you fail, the less fearful you become.

The less fearful you become, the more confidence you build.

The more confidence you build, the more your eyes open to opportunities.

The more your eyes open to opportunities, the more chances you have to make lemonade.

Switch On: Risk

The risks that you take need to be right for you. Focusing on risk or reward can lead to imperfect decisions. It's a Steady Settler or Change Chaser move. Settling for something less than your full potential will skew your trajectory, and you'll likely receive less than what you should have. When you think about risks in the context of rewards, your decision-making abilities will become sharper. Information may be scarce and transparency lacking, but if you do your homework, you'll discover innumerable opportunities to reap the rewards.

I IS FOR INDEPENDENCE

Avoid the herd mentality to gain freedom of choice

The one who follows the crowd will usually get no further than the crowd. The one who walks alone is likely to find themselves in places no one has ever been before.

—Albert Einstein

6

YOUR CAREER DEPENDS
ON THE GREEK ALPHABET

The Greek alphabet plays a huge role in the success of your career, and you might not even realize it.

Alpha and beta, the first two letters in the Greek alphabet, also are two ratios that investors use to calculate, compare, and predict investment returns. But they're also essential tools to your career success.

Here's how investors think about alpha and beta in the context of the stock market:

The beta of a stock is *how volatile* that stock is expected to perform relative to a stock market index.

For example, an early-stage technology company tends to have high beta relative to a stock market index. Since the company may have new technology or an unproven track record, the underlying company is highly volatile.

The alpha of a stock is how well that stock *outperforms* a stock market index.

For example, if you're a money manager, often you're measured on how well your investment portfolio performs relative to a stock market index. The outperformance you generate is your alpha. If the stock market index generated 10 percent, and you generated 15 percent, then your alpha is 5 percent. That point is important: alpha doesn't exist on its own—it must be actively created.

While both are financial terms, you don't have to be a stock market whiz to use alpha and beta. Here's how alpha and beta can dramatically improve your career.

Alpha, Beta, and Your Career

When you think about which career is right for you, start with alpha and beta. It's necessary to understand the "beta" of your job, but the "alpha" is what really matters. Simply put: *Don't focus on the job. Focus on the job where you can outperform.*

Alpha is all about *you*—how well you can outperform relative to everyone else. Don't just choose the exciting job or the job your friends choose. Choose the job that matches your unique talents and skills. Here's how you should think about creating alpha at work:

- Is this job your true calling?
- Are you great at what you do?
- Do you outperform your colleagues?
- Is this job the best use of your core strengths and talents?

Beta is not about you, but about *the job itself* relative to other jobs.

- What's the compensation structure?
- How many hours do you work?
- What are the employee benefits?
- What's your job title?

Change Chasers, Steady Settlers, and Eternal Excusers focus on beta; they're most interested in the job itself. They gravitate to the job with the big paycheck or at the name-brand company. If they work in the hot industry or prestigious position, they think the job itself will carry them toward success.

Daring Disruptors focus on alpha, on opportunities where they can excel, outperform peers, and create the largest impact. They're not blind to compensation or attractive roles, but for them, alpha creation begins with a matching principle: it's all about matching you to your right job. Not the job where you think you're supposed to work, the one with the biggest paycheck, or the one in the headlines.

Change Chasers are speculation seekers and beta chasers—they seek careers with high volatility. They play for the big win, and they'll throw money at speculative activities that potentially can yield outsized returns, like day trading.

Steady Settlers want a stable career and paycheck. They are happy to achieve the "market return" in a play-it-safe career. Nothing too risky, nothing too volatile—like being a lawyer.

Eternal Excusers don't focus on the work; they focus on complaining about the work. They complain about the company, management, and colleagues. As a result, they underperform peers and fail to spot bigger career opportunities. Their energy is misdirected toward bringing people down, not building people up. Career progression escapes them, and they're stuck in whatever nine-to-five job pays the bills.

Daring Disruptors focus on alpha, not beta. They don't blindly follow the lockstep career path of Steady Settlers, or chase beta like Change Chasers who want to work on Wall Street or in Silicon Valley—not because it's their passion or they were born to invest or build great technology ventures, but because they see dollar signs.

Rather, Daring Disruptors apply these three principles to generate alpha, no matter the type of career:

1. Think bigger than a typical Harvard reject.
2. Seize opportunities that others miss in the jeans aisle.
3. Apply your "edge" to scale skyscrapers.

How can you achieve alpha at work? Follow these three rules.

Think Bigger Than a Typical Harvard Reject

Jack Ma was a teacher who attended, in his words, "my city's worst university." When he applied to work in the private sector, no one would hire him.

When KFC came to his city, twenty-four people applied, and twenty-three were hired. Ma was the only one rejected. The police hired four people from his town. He was the only one rejected. He failed his college entrance exam three times. He was rejected from Harvard ten times.

You know how an Eternal Excuser would have responded to such a barrage of rejection? Resentment. Deflation. Frustration.

But Ma understood how to seize opportunities. In 1972, Richard Nixon visited Ma's hometown of Hangzhou, China, and thereafter, it became a popular tourist destination. As a teenager, Ma wanted to learn English, but he couldn't readily access books in English. So for nine years, he rode his bike to a local hotel, the Hangzhou Hotel, to meet people, practice English, and give free tours. Despite never having traveled outside of China, Ma said the experience opened his mind to a world of possibility.

In 1995, he used his English skills on a trip to Seattle, where he traveled as an interpreter for a trade delegation. There, he saw the internet for the first time. His friend asked him to type in anything he wanted. Despite first being nervous about touching the computer, for fear of breaking it and not being able to afford a replacement, he typed the word "beer" in Yahoo's search engine. The results included beers from Germany, the United States, and Japan, but there was no information about beer in China. He then added the word "China" to the "beer" search term, but still received no results. When they entered additional search terms, they didn't find much information about China at all.

To fill this apparent market void, Ma subsequently launched a website called China Pages, a directory of Chinese companies seeking to connect with customers abroad. At this point, despite not knowing much about computers, the internet, or email, Ma recognized an opportunity and seized it.

Unfortunately, China Pages failed. After leaving China Pages, Ma received an offer in Beijing to help the government promote e-commerce. After learning more about e-commerce, Ma saw another opportunity to start his own e-commerce company.

Despite not having any money, a business plan, or technology, Ma gathered seventeen people in his tiny apartment to share his vision to create a new venture, Alibaba. Today, Alibaba is China's largest e-commerce platform, and Ma is a billionaire many times over.

"Think bigger" means to think beyond your current sphere to the sphere where you want to go and the sphere that you want to build. The world is much bigger than your immediate vicinity. When you think bigger, you'll naturally have more opportunities to outperform and generate alpha.

Ma didn't speak English, but he saw an opportunity to learn English. He had never used a keyboard before, but he saw an opportunity to build an internet business. Ma learned about e-commerce in one job, and then saw an opportunity to create his own e-commerce company.

Ma represents the epitome of how to think bigger—bigger than yourself, your community, your skills, your purview—to excel.

Seize Opportunities That Others Miss in the Jeans Aisle

In the mid-1960s, Don Fisher, who refurbished old hotels, bought the Capitol Park Hotel in Sacramento. He leased space to a Levi's jeans salesman, who opened a showroom in the hotel. After Don bought two pairs of jeans and slacks from the Levi's salesman, he discovered they didn't have his size. Don needed a thirty-four-inch waist and thirty-one-inch length, but all the pants delivered from the distribution center were thirty-inch length.

Naturally, Don asked the salesman if he could exchange the pants for the right size. The salesman responded that it would be "a paperwork nightmare," and recommended that Don try exchanging the pants at a department store in San Francisco. When Don's wife, Doris, visited Macy's to return the pants, she found a messy Levi's display table in the basement, which only included even sizes with about five pairs in each size category. Following this unsuccessful experience, Don tried another department store, the Emporium, but still couldn't find his size.

"What if someone put together all the styles, colors, and sizes Levi Strauss had to offer in one store?" Don asked.

So the Fishers decided to start their own store, Gap, that carried all sizes and styles of Levi's jeans. With a target market of twelve- to twenty-five-year-olds, Gap would focus on the pants category, and sell records and tapes.

The Fishers, who had no prior retail experience, didn't choose the retail sector because they liked the job description. Rather, the Fishers capitalized on a missed opportunity in the market, which they could leverage to launch a new specialty retailer to compete head-on with department stores—and where they could excel.

Even the smartest people and most established companies miss opportunities. You generate alpha by finding those opportunities that others miss. The action is where you create it, not always where everyone else gathers.

Apply Your "Edge" to Scale Skyscrapers

Lawrence Wien started his career as a New York City real estate lawyer, opening his own law firm soon after graduating from Columbia Law School in 1927. Over the next four years, Wien wondered how he could use his deep legal knowledge beyond practicing law.

He couldn't afford to buy large properties alone, but he wondered if he could pool funds from several small investors to collect the money he needed. With this idea, Wien used his understanding of real estate and tax law to pioneer a new investment structure known as public real estate syndication, which enabled a small group of investors to acquire real estate assets that none of them could buy individually.

In 1931, Wien and three partners each contributed $2,000 to buy a small apartment house in Harlem. From that first investment, over the next fifty-plus years, Wien organized almost one hundred real estate syndicates in partnership with nearly fifteen thousand investors that controlled—through ownership or long-term leases—landmark New York City properties such as the Empire State Building and the Plaza Hotel. His holdings also included, at various times, the Equitable Building, the Fifth Avenue Building, the Garment Capitol Building, the Graybar Building, and the Lincoln Building, as well as landmark hotels such as the Governor Clinton, the Lexington, the St. Moritz, the Taft, and the Town House.

Wien's edge was his innate understanding of real estate and tax law, which he combined to become one of New York's top real estate investors.

An edge is an expertise or skill that gives you a competitive advantage. We all have one—find yours. To elevate your performance at work and generate alpha, apply your edge to something that others can't do or haven't yet thought of doing. Become the go-to person because of your edge.

Importantly, while these examples involve high-profile individuals, it doesn't matter where you work or what you do for a living. It also doesn't matter how much money you make, or how prestigious your employer is.

What matters most is whether you generate alpha at work.

So, how do you find the right career in which you can generate alpha?

How to Find Your Dream Job in Less Than Two Minutes

We often hear "do what you love, and you'll be successful."

If only it were that easy.

Do what you love ≠ Dream job

Doing what you love is part of the formula, but there's more to it. To create alpha at work, you must outperform.

To outperform, your dream job should meet three criteria:

DO WHAT YOU LOVE. You wake up in the morning excited to do this. If you're not genuinely inspired by what you do, it's the wrong job, and you'll never outperform.

BE GOOD AT IT. You're genuinely good at what you do. If there were a test at work, you'd ace it. In fact, you're so good at your job that people are willing to pay you to perform it. If you're not good at your job, how can you possibly outperform?

BE FULFILLED. Your job meets your personal and professional needs, however you define them. Choose the career that satisfies the needs most important to you, whether financial, emotional, mental, spiritual, or something else. You're in charge of defining what fulfillment means to you. When it comes to your career, there's no universal definition. To you, it may mean financial return, while to your neighbor it may mean an ability to help others. For your friend, it may mean achieving a healthy emotional and mental state. We're all fulfilled in different ways, so choose a career that satisfies and completes you. Without fulfillment, you'll lose the passion to excel at work and, ultimately, won't outperform.

When we tie all these concepts together, we have the building blocks to generate alpha at work.

Therefore, the secret formula to find your dream job looks like this:

Do what you love + Be good at it + Be fulfilled = Dream job

At its core, the formula to create alpha at work begins with two components related to happiness: "do what you love" and "be fulfilled."

Doing what you love is self-evident, but how should you think about being fulfilled at work? Fulfillment at work is deeply personal; therefore, you must create your own system to ensure that your career meets your unique needs. You can create a personal fulfillment checklist to include your criteria.

Here's a sample, although you should include the criteria most important to you:

Work Fulfillment Checklist

✓ Inspiring boss
✓ Career development and progression

✓ Fun colleagues
✓ Entrepreneurial culture

✓ Mission-oriented organization
✓ Opportunities to generate alpha

✓ Collaborative environment
✓ Matches your skill set

✓ Flexible schedule
✓ Mentorship

Only you can decide what you need to be fulfilled at work. When you do the work up front, it's much easier to check the items off your list for each opportunity.

Now that you know the Dream Job Formula and Work Fulfillment Checklist, let's look at the other side of the spectrum.

How many people do you know who are absolutely miserable in their jobs? Some may spend seventy thousand hours or more at work during their lifetime. Many people can't do something they don't like for more than fifteen minutes. Somehow, though, they're willing to put up with a bad job for years.

You don't have to be miserable at work. Too many resort to "staying strong" or "toughing it out" in a crappy job they despise because that's the wisdom they've always heard. This is despite being unmotivated, having bad colleagues, working under an unreasonable boss, creating a product you wouldn't buy, or following a mission you don't believe in. But, that's exactly what people do.

Do you want to settle for a job where you're miserable? Do you want to settle for a job where you go to work dreading the day ahead and come home deflated? That's not a life—it's a life sentence.

Why is life so bad that you have to spend forty, sixty, eighty, or one hundred hours a week at something you don't care about and that makes you miserable? Your job doesn't have to be a painful existence that interferes with your otherwise fun life. We all have to put food on the table and make sacrifices to support our families, but you don't have to live a life of misery, where work is a punishment every day. You have a choice in life. Do you want to be a Daring Disruptor who wakes up every day ready to crush it at work? Daring Disruptors aren't deterred by the amount of time they work. They don't mind working forty to one hundred hours a week because they love what they do, they're good at it, and they feel fulfilled. They're alpha creators.

Or do you want to be an Eternal Excuser who spends time miserable and complaining, where work ruins your mood, stresses you out, and puts weights on your shoulders? Which life do you want?

If you've thoughtfully curated your wolfpack, you're likely to find some people who like their job and create alpha at work. If you can't find them, keep looking. Add them to your wolfpack. You want someone in your inner circle who is inspired at work. Otherwise, you'll operate in a wolfpack of Eternal Excusers, Steady Settlers, and Change Chasers. Learn why others like their job and why you don't. Learn their formula, and draw inspiration from their inspiration.

If you want to generate alpha at work, you need a work culture in which you can thrive. Your work culture matters. Daring Disruptors don't mistake an organization that promotes hard work and high standards as an organization with a negative culture. Companies don't run themselves. Expect your job to be demanding. Expect to operate at a level outside your comfort zone. Expect to work harder than your friends. An organization built on high performance is different from a negative work environment driven by erratic bosses with poor leadership skills. Eternal Excusers conflate the two. Steady Settlers put up with both, but don't question either. Change Chasers can't handle either. Only Daring Disruptors know the difference, and they gravitate toward career opportunities that avoid bad work cultures.

If you're stuck in a bad work culture or afraid you'll miss the warning signs, remember these five rules:

1. Avoid the Jerk Pyramid
2. You Can Fire Your Boss
3. Beware the Eternal Excuser in a Daring Disruptor's Clothing
4. Your Worst Job Can Be Your Best Job
5. A Top Dog Leader Should Bark at Least Five Times

Let's see how each warning sign works in practice.

Avoid the Jerk Pyramid

If your organization's work culture is flawed, your ability to create alpha can be materially challenged. One major red flag is the Jerk Pyramid. That's right—Jerk Pyramid, which is composed of three general groups:

- Senior management (Top Dogs)
- Middle management (Middle Dogs)
- Everyone else (Junior Dogs)

Make no mistake: the Jerk Pyramid isn't a meritocracy; it's a top-down culture. With top-down cultures, responsibility starts in one place: the top. That means the Top Dogs set the tone for the organization. In a Jerk Pyramid, the problem is that the Top Dog isn't a real leader, but a jerk. If the Top Dog is a jerk and barks orders at the Middle Dogs, then the Middle Dogs often emulate the Top Dog and become jerks as well.

You may ask: Can't Middle Dogs break the cycle? They certainly can. Effective leaders in their position would. But Middle Dogs often don't. Why? Middle Dogs want to become Top Dogs one day, so they think they need to act like Top Dogs, and in a Jerk Pyramid, Top Dogs are jerks. Therefore, Middle Dogs become jerks too. So Middle Dogs bark orders down the pyramid to the Junior Dogs. Junior Dogs can't bark orders at anyone, and they bear the brunt of the Top Dogs barking at the Middle Dogs, who in turn bark orders at them. So Junior Dogs feel disrespected, disconnected, unvalued, and unhappy at work.

Hence, the Jerk Pyramid. Here it is in all its glory:

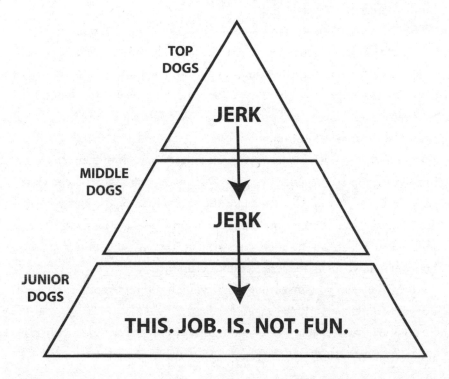

THE JERK PYRAMID

TOP DOGS

JERK

MIDDLE DOGS

JERK

JUNIOR DOGS

THIS. JOB. IS. NOT. FUN.

This is how it works, folks. Jerks at the top act like jerks to the middle, who act like jerks to everyone else in the organization.

According to *Harvard Business Review*, about half of all managers don't trust their leaders. When team members don't have confidence in their leaders, they're less willing to trust and cooperate. This is why it's critical for every organization to evaluate its culture and ensure that any Jerk Pyramid is removed.

TOP DOGS: If the senior leaders are jerks, it permeates throughout the organization like a bottle of spilled poison.

MIDDLE DOGS: Your leadership approach doesn't have to mirror your boss's management style. Research shows that the best way to break the chain is to develop your own strong moral identity that is distinct from that of your manager. You don't have to be a jerk because Top Dogs are jerks. Set the tone, take care of your people, and treat Junior Dogs with respect.

JUNIOR DOGS: If your organization has a Jerk Pyramid, it's time to rethink your career trajectory. Ask yourself: Is this really the organization where I want to build a career and generate alpha?

The Jerk Pyramid has financial consequences for organizations as well. It turns out that jerks are expensive. Research shows that incivility at work leads to a decline in work effort, work quality, performance, and creativity—all of which adversely impacts profitability. When incivility reigns, think of all the lost customers, employees, and productivity. Years ago, the cost of incivility at Cisco was estimated at $12 million.

Top Dogs, if you have jerks in your organization, remove them en masse. Don't give the top-selling jerk a free pass. Don't hang on to the jerk who closed the big deal last quarter. Don't tolerate the smart jerks or the creative jerks. Otherwise, you value them more and your team less—and it's a culture and morale killer. When you give jerks a platform, the Jerk Pyramid flourishes. When you remove them, the Jerk Pyramid crumbles.

No matter who you are or how high you climb, remember to be kind. Kindness requires zero talent.

Too often, in the quest to excel and build, it's easy to focus on a "whatever it takes" culture to get things done.

Here's the thing:

You can still hit all the deadlines.

You can still drive excellence.

You can still inspire.

You can still be productive.

You can still be firm.

You can still promote discipline.

But do it with kindness.

You Can Fire Your Boss

So, you apply the Dream Job Formula, and you think you've found your dream job. You've done a thorough check and haven't found a Jerk Pyramid. The only issue is that you haven't met your boss, who was traveling during the interview process. But being the diligent person you are, you learn as much as you can about your new boss and show up on your first day ready to go. Then, you meet your new boss, and let's just say the pool is slightly different from the brochure.

Your boss matters because he or she likely has the most direct impact on your work life, including your satisfaction at work. When it comes to your boss, one thing is certain: a bad boss can ruin a team or an organization and be your top roadblock to creating alpha at work. Like your wolfpack, the people you spend time with at work can directly affect your mental outlook, energy level, and overall happiness. They also can influence how you lead and manage others. When you join an organization, you're not just joining a brand or product. You're joining a specific team or group within that company. Your individual experience will differ from the experiences of your colleagues within the same company, even if they sit down the hall from you. That's why it's critical to focus on the team you're joining, including—and perhaps most important—your boss.

Therefore, if you have the opportunity, choose your boss wisely. For many, bosses aren't a choice. You join an organization and are assigned a boss. You think one person is your boss, and when you start hitting it off, they're suddenly transferred to the San Antonio office. You can work for the greatest company with the highest salary, best perks, and an important mission, but if your boss is intolerable, then what's the point?

You may not hire your boss, but you have a choice to fire your boss. Here's the cold, hard reality: there's no time for you to work for a miserable boss. Firing your boss doesn't make you a complainer, a quitter, or an Eternal Excuser. The difference here is that you're hungry, you're fully committed, and you're willing to do what it takes to succeed. However, your boss is a clear roadblock.

You could stick with it and hope it gets better, but hope isn't a strategy. Your life is too valuable to waste your career with someone who creates misery at work and prevents you from doing your job. This is about you taking control of your work life and finding a critical solution to reshape your path. Find a new boss, a new department, a new team, a new role within the organization as soon as possible—that is, find ways to create new opportunities at work. If your response is "I wish, but it's not that easy," or "There are no opportunities within the organization," then either look harder or realize it's time to leave the organization. However, staying in a negative situation isn't an option. Each day you wait to act is another day of opportunities missed.

The future of work has no patience for ineffective bosses who rule with iron fists and use fear tactics to lead. The future of work will bring more efficiency to teams and reduce hierarchical structure in favor of meritocracy. For the Daring Disruptors who lead and create enterprises of the future, it's incumbent upon you to set a new course for leadership. If you're already a boss, make sure the following criteria don't apply to you. If you're not a boss, one day you may be. Don't ever treat other people like this. It kills morale and productivity, and will ultimately lead to your downfall.

Here are five signs that you should fire your boss:

Sign #1: Your boss thinks that shouting is communicating.

Bosses who shout are not in control. They aren't in control of themselves or those they manage. Shouting is a tactic used to intimidate, not to inspire. Bosses who think shouting "gets the job done" or "keeps employees in line" are mistaken. A boss who shouts will never gain employees' trust or confidence. Never. It may scare some employees in the short term, but the boss will never win over their hearts and minds. No team thrives when the leader shouts. Teams thrive when the team is empowered to work toward a common mission. If the leader cannot communicate the team's mission, the team will fail.

This isn't to say that leaders cannot be firm or hold their employees accountable. Leaders are expected to do those things, and employees should expect to be held accountable. However, as a leader, how you communicate is an important measure of your ability to lead. It's up to individual leaders to find their voice. If they can't, the team may fail, and the organization will suffer.

Sign #2: Your boss doesn't really understand your business.

Whether you're an assistant manager, a vice president, or a chief executive, you should understand everything about your business. Not only your specialty or product, but the entire business.

Does your boss understand your business? Could your boss do your job? A leader should be able to perform the tasks of his or her team members. The leader may not be an expert at everything, but a leader should be able to solve problems, leverage resources, and get the job done.

Too many leaders are quick to blame their team and focus on the wrong issues. Why? They don't fully understand their business. They don't focus on what's important because they don't understand the drivers and levers.

Sign #3: Your boss is a show horse, not a workhorse.

This should be an easy one for you to answer: Does your boss promote your boss or your business? Is he or she a workhorse or a show horse?

There's a clear divide between a workhorse and a show horse. A workhorse is a CEO who lives and dies by the business, whose passion is driving the organization forward, and who wouldn't want to be doing anything else. A show horse is a CEO who's focused on promoting a self-serving image and driving a personal platform.

Show horse CEOs put themselves above the business, even though the business, shareholders, employees, and customers should always come first. Show horse CEOs and bosses don't last long because their teams and customers see through their charade. As a result, both groups lose confidence in the leader, and the overall business becomes secondary.

Sign #4: Your boss doesn't understand the culture.

A boss who doesn't have his or her pulse on the organization's culture is bound to fail. No matter where you fall in the hierarchy, CEOs and managers alike need to connect with their colleagues. They need to embrace the organizational culture, set the tone, and promote the company and its mission. This takes active listening and engagement. It's more than reading the company handbook or attending a town hall or company picnic.

Bosses who don't understand the company culture will further disconnect themselves from the organization. When they disconnect, their teams disconnect as well. That means everyone suffers, because a weaker culture hurts every aspect of the business.

Sign #5: Your boss wastes time on menial tasks and misses the big picture.

Does your boss sweat the small stuff? If so, he or she is likely to miss the big picture. We've all seen managers who pick on people and highlight small mistakes. Or they encourage inefficient processes that take twice as long to complete.

Effective leaders focus on the big picture. They understand what matters. They streamline. They honor and respect people's time.

It's incumbent upon the leader to understand the big picture, in addition to understanding the details. Leaders who understand the big picture can connect the dots. It's the leaders' job to steer the ship and set the course. When they do, they'll find that their team is best positioned to fulfill the company's mission.

And when that happens, everyone wins.

Your happiness at work matters. It matters for your personal happiness and your professional success. Don't be a Steady Settler. Settling for a bad boss is only the beginning. Working in a job for the prestige or joining a company for the big bucks when it's not your true calling won't end well. You're settling. It may not feel that way, but beneath the masks of prestige and paychecks, your professional calling is disconnected from your best self. When you adjust your framework and muster the courage to stop settling at work, you'll begin a transformation that will extend to other parts of your life.

Beware the Eternal Excuser in a Daring Disruptor's Clothing

Some people think they're already leading the Lemonade Life and might even self-identify as Daring Disruptors. You may think you're working for a Daring Disruptor (at least that's what your boss told you), who's really an Eternal Excuser in disguise. These people are a roadblock to progress: they shut down good ideas, they squash creativity, they crush the entrepreneurial spirit, and most importantly, they demotivate.

If this is the culture at your company, you'll never thrive in this environment. How can you excel in an organization where the same old way of doing business is the only way to do business? This is a place where new ideas die prematurely, and old ideas outlive expectations. Disguised Eternal Excusers don't want to challenge you to bring a fresh approach; they want you to follow their approach.

These types of bosses think they've earned their stripes because they hold a certain degree, have worked for years in their job, or have been through this before. In their mind, only they can get the job done, and everyone else is a novice who doesn't hold their credentials. They think they're taking charge, but they're leading without listening. They think they're marching the troops, but they lack the road map. They're honking at traffic, but they're the reason for the jam.

If there were more transparency and authenticity in human interaction, you would become more informed. Armed with more information, you can make better decisions about whether you want to work with this person. Maybe this type of environment is ideal for you (good luck), or maybe it's an automatic buh-bye. Information is your pathway to making more accurate assessments about risk and reward.

So how can you spot these fake Daring Disruptors who are Eternal Excusers in disguise? Doing so will help you make better decisions for your career and beyond. If you've heard any of these lines before, it should raise a red flag because what your boss says may not always match what he or she means.

Eternal Excuser in a Daring Disruptor's Clothing

What They Say	What They Really Mean
Just trust me.	I don't think your opinion matters. Let the expert take the wheel from here.
This is the only way to do it.	I don't even want to hear your approach because there's only one way to do this: my way.
I've been doing this for thirty years.	I have more experience than you. Therefore, I know more than you.
I've already thought through that.	Because I know more than you, the mere fact that I've thought through this (even though you've also thought through this) means your solution automatically doesn't work, and mine does.
There's just no way.	If I haven't figured it out yet, there's no way you'll be able to.
If it were that easy, we would be doing it already.	Thanks for your unsophisticated, elementary suggestion. Let me tell you how the world really works. If the problem could be solved with your simple solution, smart and experienced people like me would have already implemented that solution years ago.
That's good in theory, but . . .	In the real world—where I live and you don't—it's more complicated, and you obviously don't hold a practical under-standing of the real world.

Now, let's examine this from a different perspective. Do you ever speak like this? Do you get upset when someone challenges your ideas? Or are you excited by the possibility of a new solution? Think of it this way: How can there ever be progress if you're shutting down alternative views? Nothing would be discovered. Nothing would be challenged. Nothing would be disrupted. It's living in a world dominated by Eternal Excusers, where Daring Disruptors are shunned. This way of thinking is middle management syndrome. It's the supervisors and bosses who don't want to be undermined. They view alternative ideas as a challenge to their authority, seniority, and legitimacy, when they should be viewing alternative ideas as a pathway to something better.

Find the organizations and people in your life that make you better and that you can make better. You'll find the risk-reward ratio tilted more in your favor.

Your Worst Job Can Be Your Best Job

I want you to find happiness at work. But before you do, my hope is that you have a bad job. A really bad job.

That's typically not a nice thing to wish for someone, and it may go against your ability to create alpha, but in this case, it can change your life.

When you have a bad job, it's a morale killer, a creativity crusher, and a stress magnifier. It's easy to recognize the signs of a bad job. Earlier, we made a Work Fulfillment Checklist. Here, let's create a Toxicity Checklist. These are more than the attributes of a bad job—they're also the silent killers of your professional happiness. This is a sample Toxicity Checklist; your criteria may differ:

Work Toxicity Checklist

✓ Bad boss   ✓ No company mission

✓ Negative culture   ✓ No teamwork

✓ No commitment to excellence   ✓ No leadership

✓ Highly bureaucratic   ✓ No upward mobility

✓ No career development   ✓ Creativity is discouraged

Like the Fulfillment Checklist, this Toxicity Checklist is personal and unique to you. If you choose, you can assign a score to each element on the Fulfillment and Toxicity Checklists, and then apply the risk-reward ratio.

Even if your job "fails" your Fulfillment Checklist and "shines" on your Toxicity Checklist, your worst professional nightmare may be a blessing in disguise.

Think of your worst job ever. I bet you can easily list all the problems with that job. I bet you can identify the five things your boss should have done but didn't. I bet you can pinpoint all the lost revenue streams, all the inefficient processes, all the backward thinking. I bet you had a strategy for how you would have run the business, how you would have treated the employees, and how you would have created different incentives to increase morale and productivity. Don't worry—you're not an Eternal Excuser for doing this. Quite the opposite. Your worst job may have very well created your greatest moment of professional clarity. When you have a bad job, you can see everything that's wrong.

Use your bad job to know what you want out of your career. Maybe a big company isn't for you, and you thrive on smaller teams. Maybe your company lacks agility, and you need a fast-paced work environment. Maybe your work-life balance was nonexistent, so you need to find the right company culture. Maybe you don't want to work for anyone, and your bad job will lead you to be your own boss.

No matter how bad your bad job is or was, use that experience as a learning tool to make it your best job. Use it as a filter to know what you want and don't want in your next role. Understand what led you to accept the job in the first place, and if you were wearing blinders during the interview process. Then use that job as a springboard for your next phase. Finally, have the confidence that you escaped a bad situation and are stronger for it.

In his farewell speech to his staff, former colleagues, family, and friends in the White House on August 9, 1974, the day he resigned the presidency, Richard Nixon addressed failure and darkness, and what you learn from the low points in your life:

We think sometimes when things happen that don't go the right way; we think that when you don't pass the bar exam the first time—I happened to, but I was just lucky; I mean, my writing was so poor the bar examiner said, "We have just got to let the guy through." We think that when someone dear to us dies, we think that when we lose an election, we think that when we suffer a defeat that all is ended. We think, as [Teddy Roosevelt] said, that the light had left his life forever.

Not true. It is only a beginning, always. The young must know it; the old must know it. It must always sustain us, because the greatness comes not when things go always good for you, but the greatness comes and you are really tested, when you take some knocks, some disappointments, when sadness comes, because only if you have been in the deepest valley can you ever know how magnificent it is to be on the highest mountain.

As Nixon said, greatness comes when you're really tested, when you face disappointment, and when you have taken some knocks. That said, a bad job doesn't feel good. You may question your self-worth, skills, judgment, and performance. But that eventually can be a good thing, if you know how to tackle the situation.

When you use a bad experience as a pathway for self-reflection and self-understanding, the deepest valleys are closer than you think to the nearest mountaintops.

A Top Dog Leader Should Bark at Least Five Times

Take a hard look at the leaders in your organization.

If you're a Top Dog, part of creating alpha at work is ensuring that a positive work culture permeates your organization, and that those who report to you also have the foundation to thrive. That responsibility starts with you.

Start by being a good manager who sets a clear vision, defines expectations, empowers people, and provides honest feedback.

This list isn't definitive or comprehensive, but it presents the minimum attributes that every leader should embrace.

Loyalty

Be loyal to the organization, its values, and its mission. Be loyal to your team. Protect your people. Be their voice and their champion. You hired them for a reason. Lift them up with support and resources, so they can do their job and fulfill the company's mission.

Work Ethic

The work ethic starts with you. Hard work and self-discipline should govern the day. You, too, must get in the arena. Your office may have nice views, but the arena is where the action is. You must understand the big picture and details. Promote and practice excellence. Drive change and raise standards. Remember: you're the leader. Lead by example and lead the team toward the goals.

Respect

Respect is a human requirement, not a work requirement. Treat everyone in the organization equally and fairly, with respect and decency, regardless of position or title.

Integrity

Ensure the highest ethical standards. Encourage open and honest conversations. Expect to be challenged. It will make you better, keep you from becoming complacent, and elevate the entire team. You may be the decision maker, but value everyone's opinion.

Emotional Intelligence

Be empathetic. Connect with your team. Don't lose touch. Have an open-door policy. Be accessible and reasonable. Be a real person. When you're unapproachable, you miss things. Your team will keep things from you. You'll be surprised from behind when you need to be out front.

Compare these attributes with the leaders you know, with the bosses you've had, and with the colleagues you've observed. How do they hold up?

REMEMBER THIS: Insecure leaders dominate the Jerk Pyramid. They lead with their title and rule with fear. They expect, but rarely give. They demand, but rarely contribute. They want, but rarely appreciate.

A better approach is to offer reciprocal leadership:

Give and get.

Don't demand respect; earn it.

Don't expect loyalty; build it.

Show possibility to inspire action.

Show compassion to signal flexibility.

Encourage questions to promote curiosity.

Train leaders to develop careers.

When you employ symbiosis at work, you'll generate better outcomes, more respect, and higher loyalty.

The Secret to Finding Happiness at Work

If you find peace and happiness at work, your life will change dramatically. During the week, many people spend more time at work than with their family. Think about that. They spend more time at their job than with their loved ones. Yet some people still work in an environment that is toxic, hyperpolitical, or unfulfilling. They have a boss they despise and colleagues they can't stand. But some people, for years on end, will spend all this time stuck in the same job. Why? They like the money, the prestige, the commute. They don't know how to make the switch.

They're willing to trade their peace of mind and happiness for a paycheck and a job title. When they come home from work, how many people are genuinely able to leave their toxic work environment at the office? How many people can truly "shut off" when they get home? It's no easy task.

If you work in a toxic environment, you may have to bring work home with you. You may need to answer emails and take conference calls at night or on weekends. If your job doesn't require that, you still may bring home the negative baggage from your job and unknowingly let it seep into your home life. So you spend all this time at work, and when you come home to the people you love, for the little time you have with them, you may find yourself bringing your work home with you. Complaining about your boss. Fretting over a coworker. Worrying whether you'll get a promotion.

If you want to make real change in your life, put your happiness first. Not money. Not the job title. Not the commute. You.

You have the Dream Job Formula. You have the Fulfillment Checklist. You have the Toxicity Checklist. Use your results from these checklists to make optimal decisions, so you can create alpha at work. Here's an example of five common choices you may confront when deciding between the right company and right job, and the potential actions you can take:

Tying It All Together: Your Job Assessment

Option	Right Company?	Right Job?	Potential Action
1	Yes	Yes	Do this job
2	Yes	Yes, with caveats	Determine if adjustments can be made to make this the right job
3	Yes	No	If bad boss, first look for new role within company; if unavailable, consider leaving the company
4	No	Yes	Find the same or similar job at another company
5	No	No	Decide if you should look for a new job type, or if you should become an entrepreneur

Naturally, there are other options that warrant consideration and nuances in your specific situation that you can explore further. The example chart is meant as a starting point for you to think systematically about your career and professional trajectory. You can expand this chart with more options and more potential actions. The exercise is subjective, and therefore, only you can determine what's most important to you (think: fulfillment and toxicity), and the weight you ascribe to each component.

Whether you stay in your current role, find a new one, or start your own company, you can ask yourself three questions to optimize your decision:

- Can I create alpha at work?
- Do I have the potential to succeed and thrive here?
- Is this the right company and role for me?

If you can answer these three questions, you'll have the clarity you need to start making better decisions about your career. You have a choice to be happy at work. It's not like you have to enjoy your family life and hate your work life. It doesn't have to go down like that. When you find a job that makes you happy, you'll be on a trajectory toward a better outcome in your life. You have to love what you do. You should want to wake up every morning excited to do it. If not, then you need to reprogram and restructure your life to find the thing that gets you up in the morning, that motivates and inspires you. Otherwise, you'll be stuck in a never-ending cycle of frustration, resentment, and misery.

You cannot put a dollar value on misery. No toxic work environment is worth that prestigious title, so you can brag to your friends. No overbearing boss is worth sacrificing your positive energy. When you find a job that makes you happy, your ability to think clearly will magnify substantially. When you're constantly under pressure and treading water at work, your ability to think creatively is marginalized. You'll find that a happier job will yield multiple returns through self-confidence and personal satisfaction.

Eternal Excusers will say that it's not so easy to just walk away from your job and find a new one. There are no good jobs. It takes too much time to apply. You're too old or too inexperienced to get hired anywhere else.

Maybe it's not so easy to quit your job and go find a new one. After all, you need to support your family. So what do you do?

Daring Disruptors change their circumstances. You may not be the boss, the CEO, or even a supervisor. You can still have an impact, no matter how junior you are in the organization. You can inspire others and create the culture in which you want to work, even if your boss or CEO or manager doesn't.

Another question you need to ask yourself is this: Is the work I do meaningful?

Do you go home at night and feel proud about what you do?

Leading your life with meaning isn't optional; it's an essential component of the human experience. Meaning at work fosters a positive platform for you to excel. Importantly, having meaning isn't enough; you must act to cultivate that meaning. You can create meaning at work, according to Monique Valcour in *Harvard Business Review*, by connecting "your personal values and motivations to the work you perform."

Another strategy to create meaning at work is to ask yourself this: What am I going to do today to create impact and change someone else's life for the better? The answer to whether your work is meaningful doesn't require you to be a police officer, firefighter, first responder, soldier, teacher, nonprofit leader, physician, nurse, public servant, or the many other types of heroes who perform meaningful, selfless work every day. What it does do is challenge you to check yourself. Check yourself by finding a career that creates impact. Find a career that changes someone else's life in some way. That's the type of job Daring Disruptors have. That's the kind of company and career they seek to build. Daring Disruptors are transformational because they seek positive change in whatever they do.

You can create impact in any job. If you work in customer service, it's touching your customers' lives by forging an authentic connection. If you're in financial services, it's leveraging technology to make transactions more seamless to save time and avoid complexity. If you work in health care, it's developing innovative treatments to improve patients' lives. If you work at a restaurant or grocery store, it's service with a smile.

You may not work at a hot technology startup that's on a mission to change the world. Most organizations don't fit that description. Many organizations don't have a technology-oriented mission. They may not have a mission to change the world. They may not be disruptive or service oriented, even if they think they are. Some companies don't have a mission at all. What if you work at one of those companies?

It's incumbent upon you—no matter where you fall in the company hierarchy, or which branch or production facility or regional office you work in—to create impact in your company. What will you do differently, that no one else has thought about, to improve your customers' lives? How are you going to touch their hearts and minds? In what ways will you ensure that your customers' lives are seamless, easier, faster, simpler? It's up to you to be creative, disruptive, transformational—and independent. That's your mission, even if your company doesn't have one.

As you become more independent and consciously control your career, you may find yourself standing at the beginning of two paths.

The first path leads to your dream job, but you're working for someone else.

The second path leads to the job that many want, but few can master: entrepreneur.

Becoming an entrepreneur is the ultimate position of freedom and possibility. However, despite the success stories that dominate the news, it's not all upside and glory. I also want you to understand the other side.

The Job That Everyone Wants (but Not Really)

At some point, almost everyone thinks they want to be an entrepreneur. They like the glory of running their own company, not having a boss, being independent, setting their own schedule, and escaping the nine-to-five.

Do you *really* want to be an entrepreneur?

How many times have you been rejected repeatedly for one thing?

And we're not talking about the lottery for *Hamilton* tickets.

We're talking about something you worked really hard for, something you were passionate about, and no matter how hard you tried or how hard you hustled, you heard no over and over again. That's what it's like to be an entrepreneur.

Being an entrepreneur isn't scripted. It's not going to play out in a two-hour movie, with all the puzzle pieces fitting perfectly. There's no get-rich-quick playbook. The reality is that to succeed in an entrepreneurial venture, there's a lot of behind-the-scenes blood, sweat, and tears that people don't talk about. You see the aftermath—the billionaires with private jets posing on magazine covers. But you don't see them toiling away in the beginning. You don't see their journey. There might be one photo somewhere on the internet that captures "the early days." But you don't get to feel what it was like for Jeff Bezos sitting at his first desk, which was literally a door, working in his garage in Seattle with a potbelly stove, trying to build the next big company to disrupt the world of e-commerce.

Entrepreneurship is a lonely road to greatness.

People think they can handle rejection. They think if they didn't get into their first choice for college or if it took them six months to find a job, then they have the tenacity to make it as an entrepreneur.

Being an entrepreneur is about repeated rejection. This is your passion, your life work. This is your pride, your baby. And you're told over and over it's not good enough. It's not what they want. It's not what they're looking for.

I want you to meet Brian, a young entrepreneur who tried to raise capital for his new business. He and his cofounders were introduced to seven Silicon Valley investors and offered them the opportunity to invest $150,000 into their company at a $1.5 million valuation, or a 10 percent stake in the company. Two of the investors didn't reply to their email. The other five passed on the investment opportunity, citing reasons such as "not in our area of focus," "the potential market opportunity did not seem large enough," and "time commitments to other projects." Despite these initial rejections (and many others), the entrepreneurs raised capital and built a great company. Today, Brian (Chesky) and his cofounders, Joe Gebbia and Nathan Blecharczyk, are billionaires. Their company is called Airbnb.

A good reminder that the smartest guys in the room aren't always the smartest guys in the room—and a good reminder for anyone of what your life can become.

For an entrepreneur, seven rejections are the tip of the iceberg. Speak with any entrepreneur who has raised capital and scaled a business, and it's not uncommon to hear stories of hundreds of rejections. Even the best entrepreneurs are told no. Even the biggest companies struggle in the beginning. Even the boldest ideas get ignored.

Do you really know how rejection feels? Are you willing to take the hits over and over and keep going, even when people are telling you to give up? That's what it feels like to be an entrepreneur. You have a vision that they don't. There's a disconnect. You know you're right. You know they're wrong. They don't have the clarity that you do.

You have a choice of what you do for a living.

It may not be your dream job, be the job you want right now, or have the salary you think you deserve. But you have a choice to work for somebody else, or to work for yourself.

The entrepreneurial path isn't for everyone. There are a lot of reasons why. It may not be financially practical. You may not have that killer idea. You may not want the time commitment. Whatever you choose, own your career. Take responsibility for your actions and know that you do have a choice.

All entrepreneurs have a defining moment in their lives when they realize they can't work for anyone else. Kevin O'Leary, *Shark Tank*'s Mr. Wonderful, knew the exact moment that he wanted to be an entrepreneur. As a teenager, his first job was as an ice cream scooper at Magoo's Ice Cream Parlor in Ottawa, Canada. It was there that he learned a powerful lesson that has defined his life ever since. At the end of his second day of work, the owner told O'Leary to get on his knees and scrape the gum off the floor. When he refused, she told him he was fired.

"Within minutes, I was on my bicycle on my way home in utter shame and shock that she had that kind of control over my life," O'Leary said in an interview on the Canadian television show *Dragon's Den*. "I have never—ever—in my life worked for someone again. Ever. No one has ever had control over me—ever—and never will."

Years later, with cofounder Michael Perik, O'Leary launched SoftKey International, a software business, in the basement of his home, with a $10,000 loan from his mother. O'Leary helped lead an acquisition spree that made SoftKey, which later became the Learning Company, an educational software consolidator. In 1999, Mattel acquired the Learning Company for about $3.6 billion.

It's easy to want to be an entrepreneur. But what does it really mean to be an entrepreneur?

What's your niche? What's your differentiation? What's your competitive advantage?

Your schedule as an entrepreneur won't be easier than it is now. You'll work harder and longer hours as an entrepreneur than you do in your current job. I guarantee you that you'll work five times harder than you do now. When you're an entrepreneur, you're the boss, the employee, the supervisor, the board of directors, the secretary, the janitor. You're everything because everything is dependent on you. You need to have that foundation to succeed as an entrepreneur.

Almost everyone says they want to be an entrepreneur. But it's not for the reason you think.

Too many people think that entrepreneurship, principally, is about getting rich. Entrepreneurship can be a pathway to substantial wealth, but that shouldn't be the driving reason. The best part of entrepreneurship isn't financial. Entrepreneurship is about a meritocracy of ideas. The best executable ideas win. You can beat people stronger than you, smarter than you, older than you, richer than you. The only thing that matters are your ideas coupled with your actions.

If you're going to be an entrepreneur, do you think anyone cares where you come from? Do you think you're going to sell more products because you went to a certain school? Do you think your company will get a higher valuation because you have "connections" on Wall Street? No one cares. None of it matters.

Entrepreneurship is the ultimate playing-field leveler. It reduces hierarchy, seniority, and bureaucracy with the flip of a switch. It's about the flexibility for anyone to chart their own course. Entrepreneurship is about building and creating something with your bare hands. It's the freedom to develop an enterprise on your own terms, to leave the herd, and venture out on your own.

Be wary, though, of the difference between an entrepreneur and a Change Chaser. It's easy to call yourself an entrepreneur, or even a serial entrepreneur. The moniker sounds impressive: "serial" means this isn't your first rodeo. You're experienced and successful. A veteran entrepreneur. Many wear the label proudly on their LinkedIn profiles: Serial Entrepreneur. It sounds better. It looks better. It resonates.

The problem is that too many serial entrepreneurs aren't serial entrepreneurs—they're Change Chasers. So, are you an entrepreneur or a Change Chaser? Serial entrepreneurs do exist. Many are Daring Disruptors who continue to push the envelope. However, there are fewer genuine serial entrepreneurs than appear on LinkedIn. A serial entrepreneur isn't someone who has founded multiple companies. A serial entrepreneur also has built, scaled, and often successfully exited multiple companies. A serial entrepreneur is a creator and an executor.

Starting companies and then starting more companies doesn't make you an entrepreneur. It may make you creative. You may be an effective idea generator.

You may be a trend follower. But you don't get to wear the serial entrepreneurial badge because you're a founder. There's more you need to do to earn the title.

Change Chasers jump from job to job, business to business. If opportunity knocks, Change Chasers answer. Unlike serial entrepreneurs, Change Chasers only scratch the surface. When things get difficult, Change Chasers are nowhere to be found. They're on to the next adventure. However, that's where serial entrepreneurs are different. It's the period after turmoil strikes when serial entrepreneurs shine. They manage strife; they pivot; they rebuild. They fix the business model and weather the storm to ensure their business scales and succeeds.

It's easy to confuse the two, but only one is the real entrepreneur. Make sure you know the difference. This way, you're not stuck with the wrong label.

Whether you're an entrepreneur or an employee, when you lead a life with purpose and choose a meaningful career, you'll create alpha at work and harness the power of the Lemonade Life.

HOW TO MAKE $110,237
IN LESS THAN ONE HOUR

Patterns are everywhere.

It's our ability to recognize patterns that helps us to read, understand language, learn music, and even recognize familiar faces. Through pattern recognition, we can complete a sequence like the alphabet because we learn what to expect after each letter.

Consider the case of an ice cream truck driver from Ohio named Michael Larson, who used his knowledge of patterns to make $110,237 in less than one hour.

Remember the game show *Press Your Luck*?

"Big bucks, big bucks. No Whammies, no Whammies. Stop!"

If you don't, *Press Your Luck* was a daytime game show hosted by Peter Tomarken that aired on CBS from 1983 to 1986.

The game's objectives were simple:

- Answer trivia questions and receive spins for every correct answer.
- Use your spins to win cash and prizes on a large game board.
- Avoid landing on the dreaded "Whammy," which would erase all your winnings.

The square game board had eighteen screens, each of which flashed quickly with cash, prizes, or Whammies. When a contestant chose to hit a big red button, the board would stop flashing, and a selector light would illuminate a screen. If that screen showed a prize, the contestant kept the prize. If a Whammy appeared, the contestant lost everything.

Lots of excitement. Lots of nerves. Lots at stake.

Of the show's more than seven hundred episodes, none was more memorable than the episode involving Larson that aired in two parts on June 8 and June 11, 1984.

Although he hit a Whammy on his first spin, Larson then enjoyed a record-winning spree of forty-six consecutive spins without landing on another Whammy. Larson won $110,237 in cash and prizes, the highest amount won by a daytime game show contestant in history.

So, how did he do it?

Before appearing on *Press Your Luck*, Larson watched the program regularly on television. He began to wonder whether the Whammies were appearing on all eighteen squares, or only on certain ones. To check his hypothesis, he recorded the program on his VCR. When Larson watched the recorded episodes and studied the game more closely, he made an astonishing discovery. Larson found, quite brilliantly, that Whammies didn't move randomly throughout the game board, but only appeared in repeated, three-square sequences. After further study for six more weeks, he found that the supposedly random game consisted of only five repeating patterns. He memorized and practiced these patterns by hitting pause on his VCR while watching taped episodes.

For example, Larson found that squares four and eight never had a Whammy. Even better, these two squares always offered a cash prize. Larson found that square four always had the highest cash prizes, plus a free spin. Square four had cash prizes of $3,000, $4,000, or $5,000, plus a free spin, while square eight had cash prizes of $500, $750, or $1,000, plus a free spin. So if he could repeatedly land on squares four or eight, he could stay in the game, accumulate additional free spins, and keep earning more money.

The game board wasn't completely randomized, and Larson had cracked the code.

Larson auditioned for the show and was accepted. During his appearance, Larson landed on squares four or eight an incredible thirty-one consecutive times. While the show's producers and CBS suspected that Larson had cheated, they couldn't find a specific rule that would disqualify him from keeping his winnings.

Beyond securing a place in the annals of game show history, Larson cracked the game show code through pattern recognition. For better or worse, Larson used patterns to his advantage for financial gain. Through pattern recognition and repetition, Larson trained himself to perform a behavior automatically.

The underlying science works like this: in your brain, neural pathways develop based on your habits and behaviors. The more you perform an activity, the stronger these neural pathways become. After repetition and practice, these behaviors become ingrained and automatic. Think of driving a car, brushing your teeth, or even hitting a game show buzzer.

This works with both good habits and bad habits. The good news is that new neural pathways can be formed, which can lead to new routines. This means that you won't be stuck performing the same routines forever and that you have the power to break old routines, including bad habits. What's the secret to breaking bad habits? If you're like many people, willpower alone won't always get you there. Your ability to spot patterns in your life can be used to break bad habits. Pattern recognition is your ability to recognize sequences and series. The secret to breaking a bad habit is to identify, isolate, and then break the pattern. We can change bad habits by identifying individual behaviors and their underlying causes. Here are some easy action steps that you can take to break a bad habit:

RECOGNIZE YOUR BEHAVIOR. The first step is to admit that you have a bad habit you want to change. If you overlook this step, you'll never fully commit to making the change.

UNDERSTAND THE COMPONENTS OF THE HABIT. It's not enough to recognize that you have a bad habit. You must also understand its underlying components.

In *The Power of Habit*, Charles Duhigg wrote that a habit is composed of three parts: a cue, a response, and a reward.

A cue is the trigger that causes the bad behavior.

The response can be physical, mental, or emotional and is simply the bad behavior that you perform based on the cue.

A reward is the positive rush you get from engaging in the behavior.

When you fully understand each component and how they relate, you can learn how to change bad habits and replace them with good habits.

IDENTIFY THE UNDERLYING ISSUE. The underlying issue, or trigger, is the why behind the behavior. Recall the last time you engaged in a bad habit. Try to isolate the moment that triggered the habit and understand the root cause. It's not a simple exercise, so start slowly to assess what's really at play. For example, an underlying emotion or a person might lead you to the habit.

REPLACE THE BEHAVIOR WITH A SUBSTITUTE. Rather than try to quit the bad habit, you can train your mind to replace the behavior with a substitute behavior. This action step means you institute a game plan before the trigger can attack. A substitute is easier because it's a softer way to transition behaviors. As Duhigg noted, you can start to change the behavior by changing the reward. Can you find an alternative reward for your behavior that provides you with comparable satisfaction?

REWARD YOUR NEW BEHAVIOR. Remember to reward yourself for following the new behavior. You don't have to quit cold turkey and punish yourself for making a drastic life switch. Celebrate yourself for your new life choice, and take a moment to cherish what you accomplished.

Now that you're armed with a deeper understanding of how to change behaviors, let's look at one behavior that is universally detrimental to your well-being.

One behavior that many of us readily accept in our life is dependence. This behavior is not about dependence on our family, friends, or support systems. Rather, this behavior is about dependence on others for our thoughts, actions, and validation. The more dependent we become, the less we rely on ourselves for judgment. The result is a continuous cycle of reliance on others for opinions, affirmation, and even self-worth. It also represents a state of laziness in which we forgo independent thought in favor of someone else's thoughts. Fundamentally, dependence is a reactive position. We become responders, not trendsetters. We don't chart courses; we follow them. We don't form opinions; we support them.

If you change one thing in your life, gaining freedom from dependence is an ideal place to start.

The secret to achieve more independence in your life can be distilled to two simple actions: (1) put up your hand, and (2) put down your foot.

Put Up Your Hand: The Most Important Lessons That Judge Judy Can Teach You

All rise. Court is now in session.

When you enter the courtroom of Judge Judith Sheindlin, one thing is certain: facts matter.

Judge Judy focuses on the facts first. She doesn't want to hear feelings. She wants to know the facts, and she wants the evidence that substantiates the claim.

Certainly, life doesn't operate in a court of law. While the real world may differ from the vacuum of a television courtroom, you can leverage Judge Judy's approach.

Here are the most important lessons you can learn from Judge Judy and how they can make you more independent:

- Facts matter.
- Prove your point.
- Show evidence.
- Speak objectively.
- Avoid hyperbole.
- Be direct.
- Be accountable.
- There's no time for excuses.
- There's no room for exaggeration.
- Your credibility matters.

Your allegiance to the facts is also directly related to your ability to think and act independently. For instance, remember Judge Judy the next time you're in *that* meeting. You've been in that meeting before. You know, the one where everyone thinks the plan is a good idea, but you're not so sure. Do you speak up? Do you raise your hand? Of course, you *could*. But it's not easy. Are you going to be the one person who disagrees? The one who objects to the plan that so many other smart people have just endorsed? Will you be the one to leave the safety and security of your Steady Settler seat?

Too few are willing to raise their hand when it really counts. Why?

They quickly determine that the risk of raising their hand outweighs the benefit of changing minds. So they push facts and logic to the side, and quickly accept everyone else's opinions. Or they may begin to second-guess themselves: if everyone else reached one conclusion, perhaps they missed something. They assume that many minds must be right, and the lone mind must be wrong.

Here, the cue is a group meeting in your office in which everyone else shares one viewpoint. The response is silence. The reward is that you appear agreeable and don't look foolish in front of your colleagues and superiors.

In the 1950s, psychologist Solomon Asch conducted a series of classic studies that demonstrated how social pressure from the majority can force an individual to conform. In one experiment, eight college students were shown a line and had to say aloud which among three other lines was the same length as the original line. The answer was clear: one line was too long, one line was too short, and one line was the same length. The catch was that seven of the participants agreed in advance to act as the majority and answer incorrectly, without the eighth participant's knowledge. The goal was to determine whether the eighth participant would conform to the majority opinion and choose the wrong line.

Asch found that across multiple clinical trials, approximately 75 percent of participants conformed at least once to the incorrect majority opinion. This was compared to the control group, which had no social pressure, where less than 1 percent conformed. Asch concluded that people conform to social pressure for two primary reasons: *normative influence* (fear of ridicule or rejection from the group) and *informational influence* (they believe the group is better informed or smarter than they are).

It's easy to fall victim to the herd mentality. There's peer pressure. Your reputation may be at stake. You don't want to be viewed by the herd as disagreeable or disrespectful. But keep in mind that sometimes herds get slaughtered. When you're supported by facts and evidence, it's your responsibility to speak up. Don't automatically assume you're wrong because someone with authority or seniority says you are. No one wants to be the one to hold out. It's never comfortable. However, if you have analyzed the facts that support the claim, use your firsthand knowledge to state your case.

Other people's opinions are never a substitute for your own. That's the indirect route. Go directly to the source: the facts. Develop opinions and make decisions based on your read of the facts. Not only do facts make you more informed and empowered, but they also break the dependence chain because you can reduce reliance on others for information.

It takes courage to challenge the majority, but your voice matters. Remember the classic movie *12 Angry Men*? The movie takes place inside a jury room, as twelve jurors debate the fate of a defendant. The jury is ready to convict, but there is one holdout. Over the course of the movie, the holdout (played by Henry Fonda) presents facts and evidence that convince the other jurors to reverse their opinion. In the end, even those who had concluded beyond a reasonable doubt that the defendant was guilty later realized, through facts and evidence, that he wasn't. Sometimes, the power of one is more powerful than an army of many. Don't be shy or too intimidated to raise your hand. You have a seat at the table for a reason.

Telling your story, putting up your hand, and speaking your mind all take courage. The next time you're in that meeting, raise your hand. Speak up. Make your argument from the facts, supported by data. It may mean having an opinion that differs greatly from the majority. It may not be easy and may never be. You may be ignored or shut down. Eventually, if your arguments are persuasive and you understand your audience, you'll begin to build confidence, and others will notice.

Don't raise your hand every time you have an opinion. A major part of raising your hand is being judicious. According to *Harvard Business Review*, your views also are more likely to be heard by the crowd if you already have built goodwill and credibility with your colleagues. For example, you're a strong performer and a selfless team member who acts in the best interests of, and consistent with the values of, the organization. When you think independently, realize your voice matters, and use logic and reason supported by facts, you're leading the most important lessons that Judge Judy can teach you.

Put Down Your Foot: How to Stop Keeping Up with the Joneses

The second area where too many choose dependence over independence is an endless maze of misery known as "keeping up with the Joneses."

If you're looking for the single most exhausting thing you can do in your life, you've found it.

And now you must stop. It's time to put down your foot, stay grounded, stop social climbing, and stop settling for someone else's life.

If you're keeping up with the Joneses, it's a full-time, unpaid job with no end date. It's a horrible way to live, and it's an unnecessary emotional roller coaster. You're a follower. You've given up control. You're a spectator in their game.

When we apply the three components of a habit, we see that the cue is any social situation in which the Joneses flaunt their social status or wealth, and you feel insecure about your social or economic position. The response is that you take actions—financial, social, or otherwise—to create an appearance of comparable wealth or social position. The reward is that you feel validated, included, respected, and relieved that you hold similar status as the Joneses.

Ultimately, Steady Settlers are followers. Like Change Chasers who chase trends, Steady Settlers chase other people who they think represent success. In this unending game, individuality and independent thinking perish, while conformity shines. There's nothing wrong with emulating a strong role model or drawing inspiration from others. However, you should incorporate that inspiration into your own life and use it as a positive force to improve yourself.

Steady Settlers expend so much time and energy "keeping up" that they fail to make concrete changes that would bring sustainable success to their lives. They've never heard this proverb: "The lion doesn't turn around when the small dog barks." Speak with Steady Settlers, and you'll see their strained necks from constantly looking over their shoulders to see if others are speaking behind their backs.

Keeping up with the Joneses isn't a new phenomenon. Lemon Lifers have been propping up their lifestyles since at least '99—that is, 1899. Norwegian-American sociologist and economist Thorstein Veblen coined the term "conspicuous consumption" to describe the nouveau riche of the nineteenth century, who acquired material possessions to increase their reputation and social power.

In *The Theory of the Leisure Class*, Veblen noted that as consumers purchase more goods and services to maintain or achieve higher social status, society is characterized by more wasted time and money. Arthur R. ("Pop") Momand created the phrase "Keeping up with the Joneses" in his comic strip of the same name, which featured the McGinis family—the ultimate social climbers—trying to keep up with their neighbors, the Joneses.

Today is the day that you stop keeping up with the Joneses and start keeping up with yourself:

The Joneses Don't Care about You

Other people don't care about you as much as you think they do.

They have the same amount of time as you do, and they don't spend it focused on you. They have their own lives to live. It's not like you're walking on a tightrope, and the entire audience is watching your every move. The Joneses with whom you're keeping up are likely keeping up with other Joneses. Those Joneses are likely keeping up with other Joneses. So it's really one big Joneses Ponzi scheme.

The Joneses May Have Nicer Toys Than You Do

When you process the following reality, you'll save yourself years of headaches: other people have more things than you. Other people have bigger houses, nicer cars, and more money. So what? You also have a bigger house, nicer car, and more money than other people. You may not know them, but they're out there. Again, so what? You're playing the wrong game. When you keep up with the Joneses, you're stuck being a Steady Settler. Remember, Steady Settlers often think they're competing with Daring Disruptors, but they're actually battling other Steady Settlers.

Don't get tangled in their silly game. Daring Disruptors love competition, too, but they're only competing against an army of one: themselves. Widen your perspective beyond your immediate microcosm and social circle. When you do this, the Joneses will become infinitely smaller.

The Joneses Aren't Competing with You

Make sure you're playing the right game. It's called *gratitude*.

Focus on what you have, not what others flaunt. Celebrate what's truly important to you: The people who matter most. The special talent that only you have. Your unique life adventures and experiences. When you make those the center of your life, your desire to compete becomes less pressing. Don't live someone else's dreams and by others' definition of success. Achieve success on your terms.

If You Want to Live Like the Joneses, You Can

It's not hard to live like the Joneses. If you want to live with massive debt and be beholden to your credit card company and bank, multiple lenders are willing to open the floodgates. However, buying more things won't make you happy. It's a patch, and patches are temporary fixes. If you want a permanent solution, ask yourself why. Why do you feel the need to be a follower? What are you really chasing? When you focus on the "why," you can more easily reprogram your response and choose an alternative reward.

If You Want More, Go Get It

You've got it backward. If it's wealth you want, you're not going to spend your way to riches. You're doing the opposite of your goal: you're spending money without making money, thus losing money, and all in the name of appearances. If money is what you want, you need to find ways to make more. If social status is what you crave, you need to make more friends. Don't center your life around keeping up with someone else's life. That makes you reactive, not proactive.

Create the life you want with the tools you already have. Ask yourself every day what you did to move closer to your goal. Driving a nice car or buying a nice house may feel good, but it doesn't bring you closer to building a business, bringing sustainable change to your life, or developing the habits that will bring you fundamental self-worth.

Then ask yourself: Why am I living life on their terms? You may think you're one-upping them, but you're not. You're living by their rules and playing their game. You're deriving your happiness and self-worth not from your own life goals and achievements, but from someone else's. You've committed to be a follower who comes in second. The problem is that your anchor is in the wrong spot. Keeping up with the Joneses does nothing to move you toward a goal. Rather, it's a static state of imitation. It may feel as though you're moving up the social ranks as you craft a false appearance. Substantively, you're treading water, and perhaps sinking as you spend more money.

The Joneses Are Broke

If you want to admire a family that represents wealth and success, the Joneses are the wrong people. The Joneses are broke. They are less like Daddy Warbucks and more like Johnny Brokebucks. Sorry to burst your bubble. The Joneses never even had money. Sure, they picked up a few accounting tricks over the years to appear rich, so they could fool their "friends" like you. The Joneses are no different from the millionaire you're about to meet. Steady Settlers don't understand this, but now you do.

Meet the Poorest Millionaire in the World

If you've ever watched a television show like *Dateline*, *48 Hours*, or *20/20*, you've seen this story before.

The story begins with a perfect family that lives in a beautiful home with a white picket fence in a gated community. Photos of their perfect life flash across the screen. Within minutes, there's trouble in paradise. Tragedy strikes. Then, the neighbors and friends are interviewed.

"By all appearances, they seemed like the perfect family."

"There were no signs of problems."

"They had everything going for them."

I want you to meet Mike Millionaire. He lives in a five-bedroom home. He drives a Mercedes. His two kids go to private school. His family skis in Aspen in the winter and surfs in Hawaii in the summer. When you're a millionaire like Mike, life is good.

The only problem is that Mike isn't a millionaire. Far from it. Let's take a closer look.

His fancy home? He bought it with only 5 percent down. The other 95 percent he mortgaged.

His fancy car? It's leased.

His kids' private school? The grandparents make all the tuition payments.

His fancy vacations? Oh, he paid for those—with his credit cards—and he still hasn't paid them off. He's the proud owner of over $30,000 in credit card debt.

"By all appearances, they seemed like the perfect family."

"There were no signs of problems."

"They had everything going for them."

Mike is the poorest millionaire in the world—and nobody saw it coming. How do they feel now, given his big reveal? Oh, they haven't seen it yet. Only you have. That's the way Mike wanted it. He wanted everyone to think he's a millionaire.

But Mike isn't a millionaire.

Appearances can be deceiving. Everyone thought Mike was a millionaire because they saw the flash of his house and car. They saw his skis and surfboards. They saw the private school uniforms. They saw his assets, and they thought his assets equaled his net worth. His trophies represented his wealth.

Change Chaser Net Worth Formula:

Assets = Net worth

It's a formula, but it's the wrong formula.

Peeling back the onion revealed that Mike paid for his assets with substantial debt. There's nothing wrong with buying assets with debt, and in many cases, it may be the right financial move. However, you need to account for that debt when calculating net worth. That's where liabilities come into play.

So, your net worth does not equal your assets.

Rather:

Actual Net Worth Formula:
Assets – Liabilities = Net Worth

Once you subtract Mike's liabilities (his debt) from his assets, Mike's financial picture is hazy. Of course, only Mike knows that. To the outside world, he is Mike Millionaire. To us, he's the poorest millionaire in the world. Now, you may already know the correct formula for net worth. However, you'd be surprised how many people forget it when they watch others showcase their assets.

To keep up appearances, Mike is willing to spend money he doesn't have. He's willing to go into debt to maintain his high-end lifestyle. Mike isn't alone—you probably know a Change Chaser like Mike.

Until Change Chasers switch off their bad habits, Mike Millionaire will remain the poorest millionaire in the world.

Switch On: Independence

Look introspectively to identify the patterns in your life. You have the power to isolate and change behaviors to become the person you want to be.

The more you rely on yourself instead of others, you'll realize how incredibly self-sufficient you are. When you put up your hand and put down your foot, you're walking the independent life path.

Stop depending on others for the answer.

Stop relying on the majority because they're the majority.

Stop caring what other people think of you.

Stop waiting for others to determine how you get to feel and what choices you get to make.

The most powerful part of being independent is the freedom to control your destiny. It's the freedom to make your own decisions and choices. Do you know how much time and energy you spend when you're concerned with what others think and say about you? Make the conscious choice to let go of your dependence on others. It's a transformative experience that will restructure your life. You'll free up resources you never knew you had. You can direct this recovered time and energy to execute more productively in your life.

Being independent doesn't mean that you're a loner walking along a country road, or that it's a table for one. It means that you're not dependent on other people for your opinions, self-worth, emotions, and decisions. You can seek others' counsel, rely on your wolfpack, and accept feedback and constructive criticism. But you don't live your life for others' enjoyment. It's about being in control of your decisions and choices, and then about making the best decisions and choices for you.

If you're living by other people's standards and rules, you're trapped in an endless cycle of artificiality that helps other people gain influence and power over your life. Independence is not only about the freedom from dependence and the ability to think and act freely—it's also about your ability to live by your rules. You must decide what's best for your life. Other people can't decide that for you.

S IS FOR SELF-AWARENESS

Master yourself to master your life

Your visions will become
clear only when you can
look into your own heart.
Who looks outside, dreams;
who looks inside, awakes.

—Carl Jung

8

TAKE IT PERSONALLY

If you've ever visited Harvard, you've inevitably visited Harvard Yard, the historic center of the Harvard campus. In Harvard Yard, you'll find everything from Memorial Church and Widener Library to most freshman dorms and the president of Harvard's office. In the fall, the red, yellow, and orange leaves that decorate the grounds of Harvard's campus are some of the most picturesque in New England.

In front of University Hall, you'll find a bronze statue of John Harvard, seated with a book on his lap. The statue is the work of Daniel Chester French, the same sculptor who would later create the Lincoln Memorial. It's the most prominent statue on Harvard's campus. As a Harvard student, I used to watch tourists snap photos with the statue and rub the tip of his left foot for good luck.

The inscription on the statue reads:

JOHN HARVARD

FOUNDER

1638

But there's something you should know about this statue. Actually, three things—the reasons why the statue has become known as the Statue of Three Lies.

1. HARVARD WASN'T FOUNDED IN 1638. Harvard is the oldest institution of higher learning in the United States, but it was founded in 1636.

That year, the Great and General Court of the Governor and Company of the Massachusetts Bay in New England approved £400 to establish "a schoale or colledge." In 1638, the year he died, John Harvard bequeathed his four-hundred-book library and half his estate to the college.

2. JOHN HARVARD WASN'T THE FOUNDER OF HARVARD UNIVERSITY. Born in England and educated at Cambridge, John Harvard was a pastor in Charlestown, Massachusetts, who died from tuberculosis at age thirty. In 1639, in honor of his gift, the Great and General Court ordered that the school be named "Harvard Colledge." Therefore, John Harvard was the university's first benefactor. However, he isn't considered the founder of Harvard.

3. THAT'S NOT JOHN HARVARD. The statue may say John Harvard, but the statue was created in 1884, nearly 250 years after John Harvard's death. French used a model—Sherman Hoar, a Harvard law student—for John Harvard's head. Hoar later became a US congressman and the US attorney for Massachusetts.

So everything about the statue seems one way—John Harvard's identity, his title, and the year—but it's something completely different. These types of "lies" aren't limited to statues. We see similar patterns in everyday life, including at work. Think of the misdirection and cover-ups in your office. Do you notice the costumes that your colleagues wear to work? Not uniforms, but costumes: the literal and figurative ways that we disguise our true selves and feelings to conform to a way of work life, environment, or culture—even if it feels unnatural.

For example, think of the common lies that you hear every day at work:

The Ten Lies People Tell at Work

1. I don't have any questions.
2. I can do this all myself.
3. Yes, we have a game plan.
4. The business is doing great.

5. We work well together.
6. It wasn't my fault.
7. Yes, I can get it done by Monday.
8. I'd love to help, but I'm swamped.
9. I'd be happy to work late tonight.
10. Those instructions were super clear.

Sometimes, what we say and what we mean differ. Notice the dichotomy when they're presented side by side.

The Ten Lies People Tell at Work

What You Say	What You Mean
I don't have any questions.	Wait, can we start from the beginning?
I can do this all myself.	Call in the backup!
Yes, we have a game plan.	We're completely disorganized.
The business is doing great.	Slight hiccups would be an understatement.
We work well together.	Get me off this team.
It wasn't my fault.	It was my fault, but I'm not going down for this.
Yes, I can get it done by Monday.	Are you kidding me? Maybe a month from Monday.
I'd love to help, but I'm swamped.	No way I'm working on that project.
I'd be happy to work late tonight.	I don't want to be here past five o'clock.
Those instructions were super clear.	I didn't understand a word you said.

What drives some people to tell these lies? Fear.

The boss will get mad.
I'll look like a fool.

Everyone will blame me.

Smart people don't need help.

It will hurt my performance review.

I'll get a lower bonus.

I won't get promoted.

When we hold back, we may not get the information we need, all in the name of perceived self-protection. Meanwhile, the boss thinks everything is okay. There's mutual agreement on an output, but an underlying information asymmetry. Your boss expects a completed assignment, but you may not deliver because you didn't ask questions, solicit feedback, or request help.

What do you think will happen Monday morning?

Now, let's replace the ten lies we tell at work with the ten most powerful statements we could be making at work.

The Ten Most Powerful Statements to Make at Work

1. I need help.
2. I don't understand.
3. I made a mistake.
4. I don't know how to fix this.
5. It's my fault.
6. Blame me, not them.
7. How can I help you?
8. I'm sorry.
9. I need to do better.
10. Teach me.

Notice the difference. These statements are authentic and candid. They convey openness and honesty, and are clear and purposeful.

Let's compare these new statements side by side:

The Ten Most Powerful Statements at Work

What You Say	What You Mean
I need help.	I can't go it alone. I value your skill and expertise. Help me realize this goal.
I don't understand.	I listened, but I have more questions. Share more knowledge with me, so I can get it right.
I made a mistake.	I own this. I messed up, and I want to do better.
I don't know how to fix this.	I want to fix this, but I need help.
It's my fault.	I take responsibility.
Blame me, not them.	I'm solely accountable, not my teammates.
How can I help you?	I care about you and want you to succeed.
I'm sorry.	I made a mistake. I was wrong and want us to move forward together.
I need to do better.	I'm self-aware and confident enough to know the high standards expected of me.
Teach me.	I value you and want to learn from your success.

When you speak your truth, your voice is genuine, and your message has greater impact. When you say what you mean, it's better for problem-solving, accomplishing goals, building stronger human connections, increasing productivity, and fostering honest relationships. Look for the people who aren't wearing costumes or masks. Only your authentic self is required. Otherwise, you'll spend a lifetime pretending to be someone you're not, which takes a lot of energy and thought.

You'll be your best when you stop fooling yourself about . . .

the person you want others to think you are.

what you really want to do for a living.

the life you really want to lead.

what makes you happy.

not fooling yourself.

Instead, start trusting that . . .

it's okay to ask for help and feedback.

you can enjoy what you do for a living.

you can choose the life you lead.

your happiness starts with you and only you.

Why You Should Take It Personally

At some point in our lives, most of us have been told, "Don't take it personally," because, supposedly, it's not us—it's them. Right?

Wrong. This phrase is an excuse and defense mechanism to ignore what may be important feedback.

Daring Disruptors say, "Take everything personally."

When you take things personally, it's an active process in which you use feedback to improve.

In their unique way, Eternal Excusers, Steady Settlers, and Change Chasers don't take things personally. Eternal Excusers operate in the Chasm of Can't, so the notion of self-awareness isn't even on their radar. Steady Settlers do as they're told but don't internalize or process the feedback. Change Chasers don't listen to others; they do their own thing.

When you "don't take things personally," it's easy to dismiss constructive feedback, from others or even from yourself. How can you become a better person with this closed mind-set?

While it's critical to be self-aware and open to feedback, it's also important to understand what taking things personally doesn't mean. It doesn't mean sweating the small stuff and allowing everyone to criticize you. On the contrary, only you have the potential to identify the feedback that's useful for you to reach an ultimate inner truth. This process of self-realization and self-improvement can drive deeper emotional intelligence. Will every piece of advice you hear be valuable feedback? No. It's up to you to evaluate and apply your filters.

Don't only listen to the people who tell you yes. You'll often learn more from the people who tell you no. If you're a business owner, it's comforting to hear from your superfans how wonderful your product is. However, spend more time listening to your unhappy customers—they'll offer the most specific feedback on how you can make your product better. Your goal is to amplify your antennae to hear more feedback, extract the positive and constructive feedback, and process both to live a sweeter life.

Self-reflection and self-improvement might seem like newer trends, but their roots can be traced back nearly seven hundred years, to one German monk.

The Fourteenth-Century German Monk
Who Helped Reinvent Domino's Pizza

Berthold der Schwarze, a fourteenth-century German monk and alchemist, was one of the first to write about self-reflection. Self-reflection is the process of understanding yourself and using this feedback and learning to become better. Little did he know that six centuries later he'd help you enjoy better pizza.

While self-reflection often may involve a conversation with, and evaluation of, yourself, it also can begin with external feedback that you then process internally. To maximize the full benefits of self-awareness, you must master both internal and external feedback.

Let's start with external feedback.

Remember: it's solely your decision who and what you listen to in your life. Only you can filter the feedback you choose to accept or ignore. Your filter is essential to separate negativity from constructive feedback. The former will lead you to the Chasm of Can't, while the latter will take you closer to the Lemonade Life.

If you run a consumer brand like Domino's, you're going to hear all types of feedback from pizza fans and doubters alike. That's the position Patrick Doyle, former CEO of Domino's, found himself in while leading the company. Doyle may well have applied some of Schwarze's self-reflection principles to execute one of the greatest corporate turnarounds in history.

Domino's was a struggling brand when Doyle decided to confront its challenges head-on. In unconventional fashion, Doyle ran advertisements that shared the brutal feedback the company received about its pizza:

- "Worst excuse for pizza I ever had."
- "Totally devoid of flavor."
- "The sauce tastes like ketchup."
- "Domino's pizza crust to me is like cardboard."

It's not every day that you see a CEO share negative feedback about his own company in a national ad campaign.

Rather than ignore the criticism and continue business as usual, Doyle couldn't have been more authentic and forthright. He accepted the harsh feedback and listened to his customers with the intention to do better. He committed to work tirelessly to improve the quality and taste of the pizza, modernize the brand, and integrate more technology. Doyle didn't accept mediocrity or dismiss negative feedback. On the contrary, he used the feedback as an engine to transform Domino's. His creative efforts not only turned around the brand for consumers, but also fueled financial returns for shareholders.

How can you incorporate these lessons and apply the teachings from a fourteenth-century monk to your life today?

You can start by taking everything personally.

As in the case of Domino's, taking everything personally means listening to and processing external feedback to become a better brand.

It also means listening to and evaluating yourself, then processing internal feedback to make you stronger and more authentic. To incorporate more self-awareness in your life, here are two easy feedback exercises that will help you understand yourself better and then show you how to be more successful in everything you do.

Step 1: PSWOT Analysis

Create a personal SWOT analysis (a PSWOT), which stands for your personal strengths, weaknesses, opportunities, and threats. The SWOT analysis is credited to Albert "Humph" Humphrey, a business and management consultant who learned the framework at the Stanford Research Institute in the 1960s.

On a piece of paper, draw a box with four quadrants labeled with *S, W, O,* and *T,* as in the following figure.

PSWOT Analysis

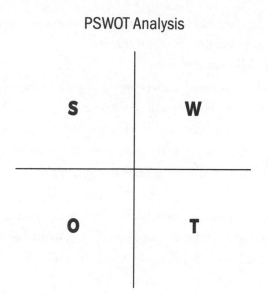

This is what each letter stands for and represents:

Letter	Stands for	Represents
S	Strengths	Where you shine
W	Weaknesses	Where you fall short
O	Opportunities	Potential areas for you to win
T	Threats	Your internal and external roadblocks

In each respective box, list your top three strengths, weaknesses, opportunities, and threats.

Your PSWOT analysis should be based on internal feedback (your own perceptions) and external feedback (from family, friends, colleagues, your boss, and others). Once you have your lists, you'll notice there's a bunch of information. For the purposes of this PSWOT analysis, the four quadrants aren't equal: the centerpiece should be your strengths. Your strengths are your backbone and foundation, and what you'll need to leverage opportunities. Determine which strengths you can apply to which opportunities, and then draw lines to connect them. Similarly, use your strengths to quash or neutralize threats, because they're standing between you and your opportunities. Think about which strengths can help thwart which threats.

What about weaknesses?

Common wisdom says to focus on improving your weaknesses. Too many fall for this trap. They spend time and effort trying to prop up their weaknesses and convert them to strengths. As if you're supposed to become this perfect superhuman. If you're chasing perfection, stop. If you think every weakness must become a strength, you'll never get there. You can't be good at everything. No one is.

Likewise, in the pursuit of perfection, too many people magnify their weaknesses, even the insignificant ones. We all have them, but only you decide how much your weaknesses drag you down. Only you decide the role they play and the purpose they serve in your life.

Instead, think of weaknesses as being instructive: they can tell you where *not* to spend your time and energy. They also can help narrow your focus. If you're not good at something, don't waste time doing it. You're infinitely more powerful when you know your weaknesses because you can direct your energy elsewhere. Focus instead on leading with your strengths to plow through, carry on, and move forward. Weaknesses don't produce results—strengths do. Therefore, all your efforts should be focused on how your strengths can help you seize opportunities.

This PSWOT is an iterative exercise that you should repeat every three, six, and twelve months to track your progress.

Step 2: GOAL Analysis

This next exercise incorporates another facet of self-reflection: the ability to anticipate outcomes, compare results to what you anticipated, and then process this feedback in order to understand yourself better. Peter Drucker, the management guru, noted that this "feedback analysis" also was used in the sixteenth century by Saint Ignatius of Loyola, who founded the Jesuits. According to Drucker, feedback analysis helps you process and apply self-understanding, so you can optimize your time and efforts.

On a separate piece of paper, make four columns, as in the following figure:

GOAL Analysis

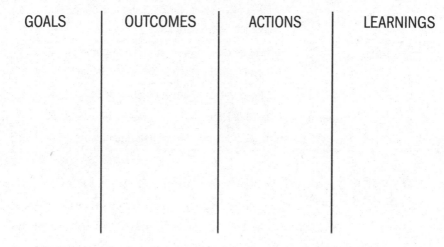

| GOALS | OUTCOMES | ACTIONS | LEARNINGS |

This is what each column means:

Letter	Stands for	Represents
G	Goals	What you want to achieve
O	Outcomes	Results that you expect
A	Actions	What you did to achieve these goals
L	Learnings	What you learned from reaching your intended goals

You should complete the goals and outcomes columns now. The actions and learnings columns should be completed three, six, and twelve months from now, as you track your progress and determine whether your decisions led to achievement of your goals. If not, reflect on why your actions didn't lead to your desired results.

For example, Patrick Doyle's GOAL analysis may have looked something like this:

Patrick Doyle's Goal Analysis

Letter	Stands for	Learnings
G	Goals	Reinvent Domino's
O	Outcomes	Drive more sales, make customers happy, and increase share price
A	Actions	Instituted ad campaign and corporate turnaround based on customer feedback
L	Learnings	Incorporation of honest feedback and self-reflection through boldness and creativity helped achieve the desired outcomes

If the PSWOT analysis is the framework to identify a road map, then the GOAL analysis is a helpful tool for self-reflection. The more you repeat these exercises, you will know yourself better and determine what strategies work best for you.

Your ability to be more self-aware will have a major impact on your personal and professional life. Self-awareness is about being more alert—alert toward yourself, others, and your environment. Let's look at an example of each and start exploring how self-awareness can help you understand more about other people.

Let's continue with the pizza theme and see how two pizza shop owners apply principles of self-awareness. See if you can determine which entrepreneur is more self-aware, and why it matters for her business.

It's lunchtime near Penn Station, one of New York City's two major train stations. Tourists crowd the sidewalks, eager to visit Times Square, the Empire State Building, and Macy's.

Two small quick-service pizza shops are located within blocks of each other. The shops are separately owned by entrepreneurs. The first shop is decorated with pristine, white subway tile. It offers an array of artisanal pizzas, with fresh, organic ingredients. The owner, Kelsey, is a classically trained chef.

Blocks away, there's another pizza shop, which offers a slice for one dollar. The decor is simple. Nothing is organic. The tomato sauce is from a can. The owner, Katie, has never taken a cooking lesson in her life.

Both shops sell pizza. One has a long line. The other is empty.

Which is which?

It's not even close. The one-dollar pizza shop is crushing it.

Why?

The artisanal pizza tastes better and looks better. It's higher quality. No doubt, Kelsey is a true artist and craftsman. She wins on innovation and creativity. Kelsey thinks that she's being an entrepreneur and sharing her creations with the world.

However, Kelsey is mistaken. She doesn't understand her audience or the location. Kelsey just wants to open her own business and be an entrepreneur. She wants to showcase her cooking abilities, rather than meet her target customers' demand. Kelsey is looking at herself, not her customers. By the time she figures this out—if she figures this out—Kelsey will be out of business.

Tourists in this part of Manhattan are on the move. They want quick and affordable, not artisanal. Simpler is better. Kelsey might have a great idea, but she chose the wrong neighborhood and misunderstood her customer base.

This isn't about the decline of the old-school, specialty mom-and-pop shop and the corresponding commoditization of the new-age pizza business. It's a simple story about entrepreneurship. Focus on what the *customer* wants, not on what *you* want. Know how to add value to their lives. Make their vacation easier. They've been walking all day and want a familiar comfort food.

Being an entrepreneur is about them, not about you. Once you know yourself, it becomes easier to understand others.

As hard as you work to look inward, external forces or threats will seek to interfere with your self-discovery and self-awareness. Sometimes, life can get noisy. How you respond to that noise may make the difference.

Beware the Chief Cheerleader of Distraction

In New York City, the nonemergency call number 3-1-1 receives fifty thousand calls each day. The number one complaint? Noise.

Airplanes. Helicopters. Traffic. Loud music. Construction. Leaf blowers.

In midtown Manhattan, noise can reach ninety-five decibels, significantly higher than the average of seventy decibels recommended by the US government. In 2009, the European Union instituted noise guidelines below forty decibels at night and said continuous noise during the day should not exceed fifty decibels.

It can be hard to escape the cacophony of life. Noise is foremost loud and annoying, but it's also the chief cheerleader of distraction.

Noise has been known to lurk inside your friends, parents, coworkers, and even your own mind. This isn't a victimless act, so it's imperative that you do everything in your power to stay safe and identify the perpetrators. Here are some types of noise that have recently been spotted distracting innocent, hardworking people and robbing them of their focus:

1. "This is never going to work."
2. "Can you really handle all of this?"
3. "There's so much competition."
4. "Give me a Q-U-I-T. What does that spell?"
5. "Spend your money over here."
6. "Spend your time over there."
7. "Hey, you should get a vanity license plate that says UWLFAIL."

Do you know what noise is?

Noise is a thief who steals focus and prevents you from achieving your vision and realizing your goals. Consider noise a roadblock on your path to success.

Are you aware of the noise in your life?

On a piece of paper, write down the five noisiest things in your life. The noisiest things aren't always the loudest, but they're the silent killers of time and productivity. Noise can be anything from your favorite website that you check ten times a day to the people who infuse negativity and doubt into your psyche.

What's the secret to not being distracted by noise?

You just took the first step, when you identified the five noisiest things in your life. When you know the things that distract you most, you'll be more likely to neutralize them.

Do you know who loves noise? Two types of people: Eternal Excusers and Change Chasers.

Why?

Eternal Excusers love noise because they don't have to focus on the problem at hand. Noise helps them play a game of perpetual deferral. Noise helps them avoid goal-setting, which provides Eternal Excusers with much-needed comfort, because they don't have any goals. They love to make excuses, and noise is a way for them to hide behind their complaints.

Change Chasers also love noise. Change Chasers are pulled in every direction because they're seeking the new, hot tip. They're on the lookout for the next chase, and noise is their go-to entry point.

It's easy to distract Eternal Excusers and Change Chasers with noise. As they're getting tricked and deceived, do you know who sits right across the table from noise?

Competition.

While you're distracted, your competitors are focused on self-awareness and self-reflection. They're not being tricked or fooling themselves. They're working on themselves, striving to do better.

So anytime you get an invitation from distraction, receive a recipe for deceit, or consider descending the rickety stairs down another rabbit hole, don't. Don't allow noise to be an excuse, roadblock, or distractor in your life.

Remember: competition sits across the table from noise. Choose your seat at the table wisely.

Noise, the competition has spoken.

If you can master the ability to silence noise, you'll be better able to understand yourself and defeat distractors. Now that noise has been silenced, it's time to focus on one of the most important skills you must master. There's no wiggle room or compromise here. This one is all about you.

You Can't Blame Sheila in Accounting

Poor Sheila. She gets blamed a lot for other people's problems.

All that noise from down the hall? *Talk to Sheila in accounting.*

Sales are down this month? *Talk to Sheila in accounting.*

Customer service didn't respond within twenty-four to forty-eight hours? *Talk to Sheila in accounting.*

The presentation is riddled with errors? *Talk to Sheila in accounting.*

Sheila isn't making any noise, has nothing to do with monthly sales, doesn't work in customer service, and didn't do the presentation. Yet Sheila always seems to get blamed.

Guess what?

You can't blame Sheila in accounting.

Blame yourself. It's called *accountability*. It's about owning up to your shortcomings, failures, mistakes, mess-ups. Accountability is missing more than ever today. There's an imbalance between the culture of expectation and the culture of accountability. That imbalance has tilted in favor of expectation, which erases the link between action and responsibility.

Eternal Excusers like to stand on their soapboxes and shout from their megaphones, but when it's time to act, they're nowhere to be found. It is easy to criticize, attack, and complain. The first question is: What are you going to do to change the situation? What are you going to do to change the circumstances? What are you going to do to change your life? Sadly, Eternal Excusers don't have the answer.

The only thing you're entitled to in life is nothing. Don't expect; give. Don't demand; ask. Don't hope; execute. Don't wait; act. Don't assume; demonstrate.

Complainers like to unite under one canopy: the canopy that lacks accountability. Eternal Excusers don't take accountability for their actions. They don't own up when things go wrong. With outcomes, you don't get to pick and choose credit. You're accountable for your actions. That's the Daring Disruptor mantra. Everyone wants the upside in life. They want recognition for success and the accolades. But you can't have it both ways. If you want the freedom to lead the Lemonade Life and enjoy the fruits of your labor, you also need to be responsible for outcomes you don't expect. If you're an entrepreneur or a CEO, you own all of it. The good, the bad, the ugly. Accountability is the measure Daring Disruptors are judged by, and it should be the measure by which you judge yourself.

You can't expect to be promoted simply because you've been at the company for five years.

You can't expect a raise merely because another year has passed.

You can't expect special treatment just because you went to the best school.

For every expectation you have about your job, you need to counterweigh it with accountability.

You know that person at work who never wants to take responsibility? That person operates in a culture of expectation, but not in a culture of accountability.

Expectation is assuming you're owed something because you're an employee. These expectations can quickly morph into complaining.

"I don't get enough guidance on assignments."

"My boss is never around."

"No one ever fills me in on the broader strategy."

Imagine that these are your objections. There's something *you* can do about each one of these objections. You don't have to wait for someone else to fix the problem. After all, they're *your* objections.

"I don't get enough guidance on assignments." Be proactive and speak with your boss to ask the right questions and get the guidance you need. It's not a one-way conversation.

"My boss is never around." Maybe that's a good thing. It can give you the freedom to shine when he or she is away. Don't wait for your boss to be present. Step up and be a leader.

"No one ever fills me in on the broader strategy." Did you ask? Ideally, your company cares enough about its employees to ensure they understand the company's mission and strategy. Ask others about the company's strategy, so you can incorporate it into your workflow.

You can't blame Sheila in accounting. Instead, learn to take everything personally.

9

ALWAYS TAKE NO FOR AN ANSWER

Conventional wisdom says to never take no for an answer. We are taught to never give up and to keep pushing despite the rejection.

While it's true that persistence can be valuable, sometimes blind devotion to one plan, one outcome, or one goal can do more harm than good.

It's uncomfortable and disappointing to hear the word *no*, but it's the "why" behind the no that matters. Don't be so persistent that you stop listening. Don't be so doggedly faithful to your cause that you ignore the opportunity to course correct.

That's why you should always take no for an answer.

Daring Disruptors differentiate themselves because they find value in listening even when they hear no—and they can pivot, as necessary, based on that feedback.

If you want to know why the no is often more important than the yes, just ask Ray Kroc.

At age fifty-one, Kroc was a struggling multispindle milkshake mixer salesman. As he traversed the Midwest trying to make a sale, he heard the same story from soda fountain owners: they didn't need a multispindle mixer that could produce five milkshakes simultaneously. Kroc listened to customer feedback to learn why. People were migrating from cities to the suburbs, and the demographic shift stifled demand. As customers dwindled, business decreased, and neighborhood soda fountains closed.

That's why Kroc was particularly intrigued when a small San Bernardino,

California, hamburger stand ordered eight multispindle mixers. A Steady Settler would be thrilled to gain a new customer with the thought of high sales potential. Kroc was excited about the sale, but he was equally curious about *why* this customer needed so many mixers, while his typical clientele wouldn't order even one. Kroc learned the answer when he visited the customer—the McDonald brothers, Dick and Mac.

Unlike the traditional drive-in restaurant, the McDonald brothers' stand was self-service, offered low prices, and had a limited menu produced on an assembly line, so customers received their orders within minutes. Kroc recognized that the McDonald brothers had created a superior business model to the soda fountain and drive-in. Kroc saw vast opportunity if he could replicate the McDonald brothers' concept across the country, with each restaurant equipped with eight multispindle mixers.

In some ways, Kroc had spent his sales career as a Change Chaser, eager to find the next hitmaker. But this time, something changed, and he became a Daring Disruptor. That "something" was that he took no for an answer—and it changed his life. Although his other customers declined his sales pitch, Kroc listened to the why from soda fountain and drive-in operators regarding the demographic shifts that had impacted their business model and reduced their need for a multispindle milkshake mixer.

Kroc understood the "why"—particularly the challenges of the underlying business model—and how it related to his sales effort. Kroc applied the same approach with the McDonald brothers, and didn't view them simply as a new customer. Kroc focused on why the McDonald brothers placed the large order, and he recognized their new business model as unique.

With McDonald's, Kroc transformed from a Change Chaser to a Daring Disruptor who revolutionized the fast-food business and became a billionaire.

So, how do you take no for an answer? Three ways:

- Don't be a fake Daring Disruptor (a.k.a. "Yay, we're a tech company!").
- Have a can't-do attitude.
- See the writing on the wall.

Don't Be a Fake Daring Disruptor (a.k.a. "Yay, We're a Tech Company!")

For every Ray Kroc who has a vision to disrupt an entire industry, there's another entrepreneur on the other side who gets too comfortable with their market position. You've seen this story before. They think they're unstoppable and can't be disrupted. They think customers will always love them. And like a self-assured boy band, they think the music will never stop.

Even when their sales begin to slip, they find comfort in their giant market share and think the rules don't apply to them. Why do they need to adapt? They're the greatest. Everyone else needs to adapt to compete with them. They're too big to fall. Meanwhile, every day, somewhere, somehow, someone is working to take them down. When that moment happens, it's too late.

Years later, that former behemoth that never embraced technology suddenly decides that they're now tech-tastic. For years, they avoided technology. No e-commerce, app, or innovation. Now, they announce their new app or "updated" website, as if no one noticed that this company has been out of the game for years. They pretend they're as nimble and innovative as their disruptive competitor.

If your business has been disrupted by a young, fresh, innovative company, you can't retroactively redisrupt them and claim that you're still the undefeated champion. You've already been disrupted. It would be inauthentic for you to try to pretend you're a technology company when you didn't embrace technology. You don't have the credibility with customers. They won't believe that you're suddenly a creative and innovative enterprise. You had years to change your business model, to make it more efficient and save costs for consumers. To show up now and try to do it once someone else has done it won't work. Consumers see right through it.

If you're a toy company and didn't build an e-commerce platform, Amazon already ate you for lunch.

If you're an airport car service that is just introducing an app, Uber and Lyft already stole your thunder.

If you're a travel agency that thinks now is the time to make your website more user-friendly, Expedia and TripAdvisor already beat you to the punch.

These old-world companies are out of business, and they don't even realize it. They're fake disruptors. They can't show up ten years late and expect market excitement for their new app. Why would anyone choose them when there are real disruptors who offer a better value and a better service?

These companies aren't disruptive; they only create artificial noise. They're holding on to a thread, hoping to ride some wave, like a Change Chaser. If they just build an app or say they're a technology company, then maybe consumers won't know the difference and will start buying their products and using their services. Maybe they can take on the startups before those new companies get too big.

Guess again. Your time has passed. You had the platform and runway to reinvent and optimize your business model. You were dominating your industry and had every opportunity to revolutionize and make things better for your customers. Now you want to change for the sake of changing. You don't have to be the first disruptor to market. It helps to have a first mover advantage, but others can still adapt if they move and scale quickly. But if you're just getting the memo that now is the opportune time to disrupt, you missed it. You shouldn't have to read news headlines or watch soaring stock prices to decide that it's time to innovate. If you do, you're a fake disruptor.

You have a right to change your business model. You can admit mistakes and hold yourself accountable. You can adapt and rebuild. But it won't be an easy trek. You have to work five times as hard to make up the lost ground, even though you held a first mover advantage and could have changed earlier. You have to rebuild trust and regain others' confidence. There's always an opportunity to re-create, but you can't raise your hand after you've been beat and suddenly claim you're a Daring Disruptor.

Daring Disruptors anticipate. They don't chase trends; they observe and analyze. They use judgment to understand how pieces fit together and where they don't. They make assessments about consumer preferences and technological innovation. They use their creativity and intuition to find a better, faster, cheaper way—all to create impact.

Don't be a fake Daring Disruptor. Everyone sees through it.

Have a Can't-Do Attitude

When it comes to being successful, what's the secret we've all been taught?

Have a "can-do" attitude.

We're taught to approach our pursuits with high energy, vigor, and positivity. If we don't know how to do something, we should find a solution. We should learn along the way. We should find a way to figure it out.

To some extent, that's true. We like people who have a can-do attitude. They put us at ease and make us confident that our request is in good hands. All else equal, we prefer the person who's willing to do the job with a smile.

What's the alternative? Should we approach tasks with pessimism and defeat? Refuse the assignment before we have at least tried? Service with a frown?

It's easy to associate Daring Disruptors with a can-do attitude and Eternal Excusers with a can't-do attitude. Daring Disruptors are the go-getters, and Eternal Excusers are the no-getters.

However, it's not so simple.

It's easy to mistake someone with a can-do attitude for someone who will complete the job successfully. However, they can be two very different people and two very different things. For example, some people are willing to do anything with a smile, but despite their best efforts, they can't complete the task successfully. You can understand the miscommunication that can ensue, and the inherent information asymmetry. From the beginning, expectations may be mismatched—that is, the person making the request mistakenly equates a can-do attitude with a guarantee that the person will finish the job accurately and on time.

That's why it's important to have a can't-do attitude.

A can't-do attitude doesn't mean you ditch your can-do attitude and suddenly become apathetic, hands-off, and unhelpful. This is not your hall pass to tell off your boss or tell your teacher to do your homework. In contrast, a can't-do attitude is about being honest with yourself, and transparent with others, about your strengths and weaknesses. A can't-do attitude is knowing when you can shine and when you can't, when you're the expert and when you're the novice. That commitment to transparency can begin with the job interview.

A team of international researchers from universities in Italy, Hong Kong, and London sought to study the role of self-verification in organizational hiring decisions. Self-verification is a social psychology theory developed by psychologist William B. Swann, which holds that people prefer that others see them as they see themselves, even if they have negative self-views. Previous research has shown that between 65 percent and 92 percent of candidates engage in "active misrepresentation" during job interviews, while between 87 percent and 96 percent of candidates engage in "omissive misrepresentation."

The researchers found that high-quality candidates who voluntarily strive to share their strengths and weaknesses during a job interview come across to interviewers as more believable and authentic.

According to their research, high-quality job applicants are more likely to be successful when they present a more balanced self-assessment. For example, high-quality teacher applicants who strove to share their strengths and weaknesses during their interviews increased their chances of receiving a placement by twenty-two percentage points. Similarly, lawyers who applied for a job in the US military increased their job-offer chances by more than five times compared to when they strove to self-verify.

Too many are eager to claim they can do anything. Whether during a job interview or post-hire, to create a positive impression, they make unrealistic commitments they can't keep. As a result, they overpromise and underdeliver. It's never easy to tell the boss no. You don't want to seem as though you're challenging authority or an unwilling team player.

However, it takes more courage and authenticity to tell someone you can't do something. It doesn't mean you are selling yourself short, quitting prematurely, or somehow no longer believe in your abilities. It takes restraint and self-awareness to admit when you are not the right person for the job or don't know how to reach the goal. There is no shame in admitting your shortcomings, and you may appear more trustworthy when you speak your truth. Yes, you may be a quick learner, and it may be part of your job requirement to just figure it out and get it done no matter what. You can remain willing to learn, while also being honest about your starting point. Find ways to support the project and show your interest, even if you think someone else might be a better lead.

Balance your optimism with realism.

Speaking your truth creates transparency, so expectations are more aligned up front. This will build trust now and minimize disappointment later. The person asking for your help should know whether you're the right person to complete the task, and whether you already know what to do or need to get up to speed. This allows you to set expectations and then adjust them accordingly. The requester may need someone more equipped, or still may want your assistance.

Too often we're conditioned to say, "Of course I can do that." It takes more courage to say, "No, I can't." You don't need to say yes to everything in your life. Have an honest conversation with yourself about what you are and aren't good at, which will help you assess where you should be spending your time and effort to yield maximum return. It doesn't mean you can't be good at new things or strive for more. It takes a more confident person to admit he or she can't do something than to always say yes.

When you have the confidence to admit your shortcomings, you have unlimited freedom. Understanding your weaknesses will help you avoid many wrong paths in life. It's not about demotivation, not believing in yourself, or having a bad attitude. It's about a realization and self-awareness of who you are and how to leverage your strengths to achieve your destiny.

Don't default to a can-do attitude because that's what you think you're supposed to do if you want success. Be more thoughtful and authentic by embracing a can't-do attitude. A can't-do attitude is about exercising judgment and restraint, while also managing expectations. You'll understand yourself better and appear more trustworthy.

Knowing when to turn on your can-do and can't-do attitudes will help you achieve more balance and ultimately make you more reliable when it counts most.

See the Writing on the Wall

Do you remember the last time you received negative or constructive feedback?

It may have been something you didn't want to hear, it may have come as a surprise, or you may have disagreed with the content. You're not alone in your reaction. When we receive feedback that we don't want or like to hear, the natural reaction may be to shun the feedback or attack the person who delivers it. It's human nature to assume the defensive position and dismiss what we think is incongruent with our own perceptions. According to researchers at Ohio State University, this is because the human brain reacts more strongly to negative stimuli. It's called the *negativity bias*, which is the idea that negative thoughts, emotions, or interactions have a greater impact on psychological state than positive or neutral ones.

The next time you receive constructive feedback, I want you to take an alternative approach. Listen to the feedback and seek the underlying message. Often, the message you need is written on the wall.

Let's use the example of an entrepreneur pitching a new venture to an investor. Every day, investors hear all kinds of pitches, most of which are rejected for one reason or another. Here are some of the most common reasons investors pass on even the best ideas. Notice the difference between what the entrepreneur hears and what the entrepreneur should hear.

What the Investor Says	What the Entrepreneur Hears	What the Entrepreneur Should Hear
"The market is too crowded."	The investor thinks there's too much competition.	"You haven't shown me why your idea is better than your competitors."

Investors are keenly aware of the market landscape. It's likely that your idea, in some form, already has been replicated by someone else. Many markets are oligopolies. For your venture to succeed in an existing market, you must convince an investor of both how and why your company will grab market share from your competitors.

The entrepreneur hasn't shown how the idea is different. What's the differentiation advantage? Does the entrepreneur know each competitor's strengths and weaknesses? Where are they most vulnerable? How will this venture take away their market share? How much will it cost to do that? The entrepreneur's idea may be differentiated, but part of raising money is convincing and persuading someone else to see what you see.

What the Investor Says	What the Entrepreneur Hears	What the Entrepreneur Should Hear
"I've seen this idea a dozen times."	The investor thinks the idea has been done before.	"You haven't shown me why all these other smart people failed, and why you're the right person to solve this problem."

Many new inventions are solutions to unsolved problems, so ingenuity arises from other people's failures. There's a reason the investor feels this way. You have to educate him or her about how your approach is different. You also should identify who tried to solve this problem, what they did, why they failed, and why your approach is better. Show the why behind your process. Give them a reason to believe in you.

What the Investor Says	What the Entrepreneur Hears	What the Entrepreneur Should Hear
"The market is too small."	The market is too small, so there aren't enough customers to scale the business.	"Show me why the market is larger than I think it is. Demonstrate how you can scale this business to a large customer base."

Educate the investor on why he or she misunderstands the market size. Break down the customer and market segments. Show the potential customer market, the competitive landscape, and revenue potential. Demonstrate who the target customers are and why they'll spend money to buy your product or service.

What the Investor Says	What the Entrepreneur Hears	What the Entrepreneur Should Hear
"I wouldn't buy this product."	The investor dislikes the product.	"There are reasons I wouldn't buy this product. Do you know what they are?"

If you were a customer and not someone with a financial interest, would you buy your product? Would you buy ten of them? You have to understand why they don't like the product. Is it design, functionality, utility, price? Are they missing something, or are you missing something? Understand the why behind the objections, and reflect on whether the product can be improved or is unmarketable.

What the Investor Says	What the Entrepreneur Hears	What the Entrepreneur Should Hear
"It's just too early."	The investor wants me to spend more money on proof of concept.	"Your idea sounds half-baked."

This isn't about an early-stage investor versus a later-stage investor. This is about any investor, all else equal, not seeing the value proposition regardless of enterprise stage. Is your idea fully baked? Have you flushed out in detail why this idea is a winner? Is your company only a product, or does it have a real business model?

Having a product isn't a business. You need a way to make money. If you're an entrepreneur, always strive to understand how a company makes money. What business are they really in? Do they own the product or license the product? Are they a restaurant operator, or a real estate investor who owns restaurant assets?

The dichotomy between what we hear and what we should hear can be informative. When we open our eyes and ears, we can learn to take no for an answer. We can process feedback, even when negative or constructive, and use it to our advantage to retool and improve. It's free, valuable advice that can help create progress in your life.

Twenty Questions That Will Change Your Life

Leading the Lemonade Life is about taking actions, but before jumping in, it's helpful to look inward and self-reflect. This enables us to reshape our outlook and reframe our goals. It's an essential exploration to help achieve a sweeter life.

Here are twenty questions that will change your life:

1. Where are you now?

Take a long, hard look in the mirror. What do you see? Do you see someone who has everything figured out, who is living the life you were meant to live, and is now the person you always aimed to be? Or do you see someone who hasn't yet reached his or her full potential?

No matter which answer fits you best, I want you to make two lists.

One list should contain all the things in your life that you think are going great for you—for example, your family, a relationship, or something that makes you feel proud.

The other list should contain the roadblocks in your life that are holding you back. It can be your outlook, your wolfpack, or something else you would change.

Take the first list and congratulate yourself for what you've accomplished. Take pride in your achievements. Celebrate your happiness. Often, we focus on the tough parts of life and don't spend enough time celebrating what's right in our lives. Take that moment now.

Now reread the second list. Anything missing? It's okay if there is. Add anything you left off that list.

When you look introspectively, you shine a mirror on your life to take an honest assessment. When you memorialize your roadblocks on paper, you see them more clearly and can express them aloud. Study them and see which ones, if not all of them, can be addressed proactively. You can only tackle problems when you see them in front of you.

Understanding where you are now—achievements and roadblocks—is your first step to finding the direction you need to travel.

2. What are you hiding?

Hiding isn't about burying a treasure in your backyard. Hiding means suppressing your goals, aspirations, and feelings. It's about hiding things from yourself that otherwise should be at the forefront. When you suppress these, you limit your potential because you don't connect your thoughts to your actions.

Growth begins with writing down your goals, aspirations, and feelings. Share them proactively with yourself. Review your list daily. Read your list aloud, so you listen to yourself.

When you record, verbalize, and share your goals, aspirations, and feelings, you can create the impetus to act.

3. What's holding you back?

What's holding you back from accomplishing every dream you have in your life?

The ultimate answer should be nothing. There should be no barriers between where you are today and where you want to be. Of course, asking yourself this question won't make you a Daring Disruptor overnight. There may be certain limiting factors in your life that you can't control. However, you can identify the parts of your life you are able to control. You need to identify the excuses you're making in your life today: *I didn't go to a fancy school. There are no opportunities where I live. I have a family now. I'm not as smart as everyone else.*

These excuses are barriers between dreams and actions. Identify your own. Understand them. Determine and implement a strategy to either eliminate, reshape, or rethink each excuse. It doesn't matter where you went to school or how smart you think everyone else is. What matters is your ability to find and execute solutions.

4. What will you conquer this week, this month, and this year?

Dreams and goals are a great start, but it's action that helps you achieve them. You need a game plan for life. Your game plan should have time increments: this week, this month, and this year.

When you conquer, you win. You're not just accomplishing a task—you're scoring and winning the game. Paying down your debt is a good example. What is your weekly, monthly, and annual plan to pay down your debt? Do you know how much you're going to pay? Do you know where the money will come from? Will you stretch this month and make an extra payment? Most important, do you know why you're in debt and what habits led you there?

Refresh your list as your goals change, and you earn more wins.

5. Who is the real you?

How well do you know yourself?

When you know yourself, you connect the tools you have with the life you want to lead. Understand and embrace your uniqueness. Don't be someone you're not. Don't be who your friends or family think you should be. Be you—your authentic, imperfect self.

When you truly understand yourself and stop pretending for the sake of others, you open yourself to a world of unlimited freedom and independence.

6. If you could change one thing in your life, what would it be?

What's missing? What do you need in your life that you don't have? Whatever that something is—feeling more fulfilled, changing your outlook, getting a better-paying job, living somewhere new, making better decisions— don't just dream it.

It's nice to have a wish list, but wish lists are for holidays and birthdays. If you want to make real change in your life, you need to develop a path toward empowerment.

7. What is your life's purpose?

Research shows that having a life purpose can help you outlive your peers and lower your risk of death by 15 percent. People with a sense of purpose also report higher income and net worth and are more likely to improve their financial profile over time. Think about your life mission. If you don't have one, answer these two questions: Why are you here? What unique gift do you have that you can share?

When you combine your unique gifts and share them with others, you can create something larger than yourself. For example, you could inspire in the classroom, create impact in business or public service, serve in the military, or raise a family with love and commitment.

Know your life purpose. Start with "My mission in life is . . ." Keep it close and at the forefront. Live it every day. Having a life purpose won't completely shield you from turbulence and stress, but it can help you weather challenges. It will provide meaning and direction and guide you toward the Lemonade Life. In contrast, Lemon Lifers don't know their life purpose. Their daily life is disconnected from any larger mission. As a result, they coast through life without a game plan or grounding.

8. If you could achieve anything in life, what would you do?

What's your number one life goal? Imagine you can do anything. No barriers, no excuses. This is your passion, your dream. It can be starting your own business. Becoming a CEO. Even running the New York City Marathon. This is no longer "I wish" or "I hope." This is "I will." When we hope for things, we let doubts get between vision and realization. When we "will" a goal, we clear the path, so it's easier to accomplish.

9. What did you learn today, this week, and this month?

Achieving the Lemonade Life is about perpetual learning.

Each day, you should strive to learn something new. Not one and done, but you should learn throughout the day. Ask questions. Probe. Absorb information. At the end of each day, reflect on the day's learnings. If you can repeat this each day, each week, and each month, you will become more empowered. When you are empowered, you can make more informed decisions with confidence.

10. What did you learn from your last mistake?

You should look forward to mistakes.

This statement is counterintuitive because we spend so much time trying to avoid mistakes. This doesn't mean to seek them out. It means that when mistakes happen—and it's okay if they do—that you transform them into learning opportunities. Think back to the last three mistakes you made. Why did they happen? What caused them? Reflect on the answers to these questions. Now, ensure you know why and how you'll avoid the same mistakes again.

11. When is the last time you created impact?

Think back to the last time you created impact.

Impact isn't only a result. Impact is a strong, lasting effect. Lemon Lifers can achieve results. But achievements by themselves are limiting. It's akin to checking the box. Lemonade Lifers create lasting effects when they achieve results. These two concepts, results and impact, should be intertwined in your thinking. Don't just focus on the achievement. Achievements aren't the end point. It's what comes after the achievement, and the effect that achievement has going forward.

12. When is the last time you changed someone's life?

It's a powerful feeling to change someone else's life in a meaningful way.

In the process, you create a deep bond with another human being and will feel a sense of deep satisfaction. It's critical that you find these opportunities because they'll make you a better person. It can be a small change or a big one. When you achieve the Lemonade Life, share it with others. Teach them. Empower them. Share your knowledge and passion.

13. What are your values?

Having a set of core values is central to leading the Lemonade Life.

Think of the principles you want to guide your life. If you have trouble listing them, think of the values your parents, your grandparents, or other important people in your life have taught you. If you have children, think of the values you want them to accept and follow. Some values to consider include honesty, compassion, loyalty, authenticity, curiosity, happiness, optimism, self-respect, and trustworthiness. There are countless others. Look inward to determine what's important to you. Ask your friends, family, and others you admire what values they follow in their lives.

Write down three words that you wish would define you. Hold yourself accountable to these three ideals. Read them every morning to inspire you to lead your life with purpose. Look at them throughout the day to remind yourself of your greatness. Review them each night, knowing that tomorrow is another day, which is one step closer to your goals. Your character shouldn't be an accident or something that happens to you. Decide who you are, who you want to be, and what your fundamental character is. Don't do anything that compromises those three things.

14. What brings joy and laughter to your life?

You need laughter and joy to infiltrate your life. Smile more. Laugh out loud. Share that laughter with those close to you. One of the best ways to make new friends in life and in business is to share a laugh, which can bring people together.

15. How can you win?

Think back to a time when you won in life.

It can be anything. Your Little League game. Your childhood piano recital. Your admission to medical school. The big client account. Now, dig deep and remember how you felt when that happened. Channel the feelings of victory. Get in a zone of success. Go back to that place, and relive the emotions. Reenter the same mind-set of that moment. Identify the trigger that got you pumped to win. This will give you more confidence to win again.

Reflecting will help you carry past success to future wins. Remember what you did well when you won: how you played, what steps you took, what you said. Bring forth that combination to the present and apply it to your next challenge. You can condition your mind to replicate those positive feelings of energy and success so that you can win again.

16. Do you control your life path?

Are you driving your life forward? Or is life pulling you along? It's easy to get stuck and let your life dictate your next move. Make the conscious switch. Lemonade Lifers are in the driver's seat and navigate their own journey. Otherwise, it will feel as though you're on someone else's journey, not your own.

17. Are you a doer (Daring Disruptor) or a sayer (Change Chaser)?

Sayers talk about what they are going to do. Doers do it. Sayers are on the sidelines. Doers are on the field. Sayers tell stories. Doers create stories.

18. Who is your mentor?

Find someone in your life you truly admire. Ask for counsel. Invite him or her into your wolfpack. The person will likely help you and be honored that you asked. Make mentors your partners on your journey. Learn their mind-set and outlook. Emulate their values and drive. Study their behavior and actions. Share your progress and offer to help them. A symbiotic mentor-mentee relationship is the best combination because both of you are engaged and invested in each other's success and fulfillment.

19. What is your legacy?

What will you be remembered for? What mark do you want to leave? Did you do right by yourself and your family? Did you accomplish everything you always wanted to? Legacies aren't just for celebrities, public servants, philanthropists, and athletes. Think about your legacy and how you will create one. It will help point you in the direction of the Lemonade Life.

20. If not now, when?

What are you waiting for? What will be different one year, three years, five years from now?

You can be a Steady Settler and plan and plan, and tweak and tweak, and run analyses, and test scenarios. It's good to plan, but overplanning and dreaming can turn into procrastination. Remember: it's all about execution.

No amount of preparation or planning can provide certainty. You'll have imperfect information. There may be bugs in the system. It may never be the right time.

You can wait for a better day, but that better day may not come. Or it may come, but the day may be different than you envisioned. You can roll the dice and wait. Or you can dive in and act now. The sooner you act, the more time you have to achieve and create impact.

Even if you're afraid. Even if you have doubts. Even if you're unsure.

Switch On: Self-Awareness

You can't do anything well if you don't understand yourself. Without self-understanding, your greatest roadblock is you.

Self-awareness is the biggest self-esteem builder. When you know who you are, navigating life becomes much easier. When you understand your likes, your dislikes, what lifts you up, what drags you down, what motivates you, what deflates you, you're able to fit the pieces of your life together in such a way that optimizes your actions and emotions.

Self-awareness must also come with self-compassion. You don't need to be down on yourself for the sake of self-improvement. Self-feedback and introspection are pathways to betterment and optimal performance. But never let self-awareness stand in the way of self-compassion. Change within you only comes when you love yourself.

M IS FOR MOTION

Make lemonade to change your circumstances

It does not matter how slowly you go as long as you do not stop.

—Confucius

10

NEVER HAVE A BACKUP PLAN

What's your backup plan?

Do you have one?

What will you do if your fortunes change? What will you do if this job doesn't work out? What will you do if your new house isn't your dream home?

Quite simply, a backup plan is your fallback position. If plan A doesn't work, there's always plan B. It's human nature to plan and think through possibilities. You don't have to be good at math to calculate the permutations and combinations of your life.

Eternal Excusers don't have backup plans because Eternal Excusers lack vision and clarity. If they can't look forward, it's unlikely that they've even considered a backup plan.

Change Chasers scoff at backup plans. They're so sure that the next big thing is the next big thing, there's no need to plan. For them, a backup plan is a waste of time because they only see the upside. So why think about the downside?

Having a backup plan is a Steady Settler move: protect yourself and have something to fall back on in case this fails. Steady Settlers are planners. They have planned all their life to be where they are today. Their lives have moved in lockstep formation as they ticked off each box along the way. Calculated and ready. And now they are here, settled.

So, should you have a backup plan? After all, it's common wisdom.

If you want to be a Daring Disruptor, the answer is no.

Never have a backup plan.

First, let me tell you what this doesn't mean. Not having a backup plan isn't about being lazy or failing to plan. It doesn't mean quit your job today and start a business tomorrow without a safety net. Not having a plan B doesn't mean you can't buy insurance or hedge your bet to shield you from rough patches and unexpected hits. You should prepare for the future, plan for retirement, and invest in your children's education. You should be one or two steps ahead, because things don't and won't work out. The deal will collapse at the eleventh hour. You'll get outbid on your dream home. This isn't about having a negative outlook. It's about reality. These things will happen.

If you truly want to crush your goals without looking back, then ditch your backup plan.

Why? You won't be fully invested in what you're doing. You won't dedicate the time and resources necessary to be all in. You're telling yourself up front that this plan is temporary. You're half in.

If you want to lead the Lemonade Life, there's no route other than plan A. Plan A is where drive, determination, and purpose live. Plan A is where you thrive and where you make your mark on the world. It's where you create impact and touch others' lives.

Plan B is where worries, doubts, and safety lurk. Plan B is about settling; it's not your first choice, and you know it. Plan B is about compromise—compromising your full potential for something less. Plan B is about regret, living a life of what-ifs.

When you have two plans, plan A and plan B, you've convinced yourself that either outcome is a possibility. When you only have plan A, there's only one possibility and one outcome. There are no backups, no alternatives.

If you have a backup plan, you're making a conscious choice to settle for a life you don't want. You won't be happy with or take pride in plan B. You won't be fundamentally fulfilled. You won't be as passionate or hungry as you were with plan A.

Too often, plan Bs get conflated with adaptability. Life is about ups and downs. Life brings setbacks, and there are too many twists and turns to only have one option. What about flexibility, adaptability, and change? When things don't work out, you need options, right?

Not having a plan B doesn't mean you can't adapt if plan A doesn't work out immediately. Circumstances change, so you can still evaluate alternatives along your plan A journey and make a judgment call at that time. But having a standing reservation with plan B may be a recipe for half effort. Chances are plan A may not work out the first time or the second or third. You don't have to operate in a vacuum. You can still pivot, tweak, and mold plan A. Having only a plan A requires you to adapt and test and hypothesize until you find the formula and scalable business model that works.

It's easy to dismiss someone who has a singular focus as a person who's wearing blinders and not opening their eyes to the world around them. It's easy to dismiss them as closed-minded and opposed to a diversity of ideas. Yes, it's situation and circumstance specific, and some people have their heads buried and are on an endless path to nowhere. But I'd rather bet on someone with the singular focus because that person will find a way, somehow, somewhere, to make it happen.

Chances are you'll stumble on your path of execution of plan A and fail along the way. If plan A is your only option, it forces you to get back on your feet until you make it happen. With plan B, you've got one foot in either door—and plan B is the one waiting with a warm bed and a delicious dinner on the table.

Professors Katherine Milkman and Jihae Shin have studied plan Bs and found that having a plan B can hurt your chances of success, and that preparing one can increase your odds that you will need it. Milkman and Shin found that even thinking about a backup plan can result in you putting forth less effort to achieve a primary goal.

When there's only a plan A, you're your own startup. You're hypothesizing and testing to find the right business model. You may tweak your business model, pivot repeatedly, build and tear down, and try different strategies. But those aren't plan Bs. They are part of the struggle, and part of your essential journey to lead the life you want.

Daring Disruptors don't have backup plans. They have adaptability plans. If necessary, they adapt plan A, rather than abandon it.

Just ask Tyler Perry, Sylvester Stallone, and the plebes of the US Naval Academy. They're all in.

I Know I've Been Changed

An episode of *Oprah* helped change Tyler Perry's life.

It was simple, yet profound advice: write down your thoughts about difficult experiences, and this will help you achieve personal breakthroughs. So began Perry's journey to help heal his soul from a tumultuous childhood. Raised in New Orleans and one of four children, Perry suffered years of physical and verbal abuse from his father. At sixteen, Perry attempted suicide.

Tyler Perry wrote his first musical, *I Know I've Been Changed*, based on his cathartic letters to himself, which he wrote to help heal his soul. The musical touched on personal hardship, but also addressed forgiveness and redemption.

After years of unfulfilling jobs, Perry became intent on making *I Know I've Been Changed* a success. He was so focused on his success that he was willing to risk everything to launch his career. He spent his life savings, $12,000, to rent a theater in Atlanta to debut his show, in which he starred, directed, and produced.

Only thirty people showed up the first weekend. The show was a colossal bomb.

But Perry knew the show must go on.

Undeterred, and because he believed in the show's message, he worked odd jobs for years and at times slept in his car so that the show could keep running. He reworked the production and tried to showcase the play in other cities, to no avail.

His mother begged him to come home to New Orleans and find a regular job. He could have chosen that backup plan. But he was still all in and didn't want to find a regular job. He wanted a job with purpose.

Finally, six years after the play's unsuccessful debut, Perry launched another production of the show in the House of Blues in Atlanta. This time, he recruited choir members and pastors from churches to join the production.

Nervous on opening night, he had doubts about whether the play would flop again.

"It was at that moment," Perry later told *Biography*, "I heard God's voice just as clear: 'I tell *you* when it's over. You don't tell *me* when it's over.'" Perry then looked at the window and saw a line of people around the corner, waiting to get inside. "I still get chills thinking about it."

Finally, a hit.

I Know I Have Changed became Perry's springboard on his path to Daring Disruptor as an A-list writer, director, producer, and actor. Perry not only refused to quit, but also was willing to go all in to make it happen. There was no backup plan. He was going to make it, no matter how much money he had, how much he lost, how much money he didn't make, or where he slept. Tyler Perry found his greatest talent when he looked inward. He found his calling when he ditched his backup plan.

Eye of the Tiger

Sylvester Stallone had $106 in the bank.

His wife, Sasha, was pregnant. He couldn't afford the rent. His car broke down. He was struggling as an actor.

He'd appeared in a few films (*Capone, Death Race 2000, The Lords of Flatbush*), but his career was going nowhere. Stallone felt he had been typecast in darker roles as a thug or criminal.

He wondered if he could write his own story, literally and figuratively. Could he write his way out of his tough position in life? He tried screenwriting and wrote several scripts. He sought to write something that could convey "the soul of a character underneath the rough exterior."

It was during this rough patch that his life changed inside a movie theater, but not for the reason you might think.

He wasn't watching a film, but a boxing match between Muhammad Ali, the heavyweight champion, and Chuck Wepner (nicknamed the Bayonne Bleeder for his hometown of Bayonne, New Jersey, and his tendency to need stitches after a fight). Here was a boxing match between the greatest fighter of all time and a local challenger who didn't stand a chance.

But Wepner, the thirty-to-one underdog, stunned the crowd in the ninth round when he knocked down Ali, marking only the third time in Ali's career that he had been knocked down. For that one moment, the underdog became the champion. David had knocked down Goliath.

Although Ali eventually won the fight, winning by technical knockout in the fifteenth round, something clicked for Stallone. He was mesmerized that Wepner almost went the distance with the heavyweight champion of the world, even if he lost the fight. Stallone couldn't stop thinking about this fight he'd witnessed.

After finishing an audition for an acting role, Stallone turned to the producers, Bob Chartoff and Irwin Winkler, and mentioned he had a script he thought they'd like. Producers get pitched that same line all the time, but they surprisingly told Stallone to bring his script by later that day. The script was called *Paradise Alley*. They liked his writing, but they didn't want to make the movie. The producers said they were thinking of making a boxing movie. Stallone then said he had a perfect story and asked if the producers would read the script if he wrote it. They agreed.

Inspired, Stallone wrote the original script for *Rocky* with a BIC pen on notebook paper, in three and a half days. He sent the script, now about eighty pages, to Chartoff and Winkler. They loved the script and, after several rewrites, told United Artists, the movie studio, that they wanted to make the film. *Rocky* is the iconic story of an underdog amateur boxer, Rocky Balboa, who stuns the world by going fifteen rounds with the heavyweight champion, Apollo Creed. It's an inspirational everyman story that injects hope and motivation into anyone who has seen the film—even an Eternal Excuser.

In a Hollywood movie, this is where happily ever after normally would kick in. However, in real life, this is when drive, motivation, and unrelenting commitment to success must carry you over the finish line. This is the moment when Daring Disruptors separate themselves from the pack.

Here, it's what Stallone *didn't do* that makes him a Daring Disruptor.

Stallone had written *Rocky* for one lead actor: himself. He likened it to a tailored suit made specifically for him. He knew he would never get another opportunity like this. United Artists liked the script. They liked the story. But they wanted a brand-name actor to star in the movie. Could you blame them? Here was a golden script, and naturally they wanted a big star to carry the film. Perhaps Robert Redford, Burt Reynolds, Ryan O'Neal, or James Caan. Stallone was unknown and wouldn't drive ticket sales like other actors could.

After repeated pushback, United Artists finally agreed to consider Stallone. Before greenlighting the movie, United Artists executives in New York screened *The Lords of Flatbush* to see Stallone's acting chops. They had no idea what Stallone looked like. After the screening, one of the executives, Arthur Krim, told another executive, Eric Pleskow, that he liked the film but didn't understand why the Italian actor was blond. Pleskow responded that Italians can be blond too. The executives thought that the blond Perry King, another actor in *The Lords of Flatbush*, was Stallone. Confident in what they saw from King, they greenlit *Rocky* with Stallone as the lead.

When they later learned that they had confused King for Stallone, and that the latter would be playing Rocky, they called the deal off. United Artists then sent Stallone a new offer for his script, this time with one condition: that he wouldn't star in the film.

So, a Hollywood studio wanted to buy Stallone's script. He was down-and-out. He desperately needed money. For most people, that would've been a no-brainer. Sell the script, collect the windfall, and use the cash to get back on your feet. A Steady Settler or Change Chaser would have sold the script.

Stallone said no. He refused to sell the script unless he could play Rocky.

No matter how much the offer increased—at one point, it was reportedly more than $300,000—Stallone still wouldn't budge.

Why? He was willing to risk everything. He was willing to put everything on the line. There was no backup plan, no other movie role, no other big break. This was his ticket.

Stallone finally convinced producers that he was the right choice to play Rocky. Chartoff and Winkler then lowered the production budget below a million dollars, which gave them, and not United Artists, final approval for casting Stallone.

Stallone stood his ground. He believed so much in the project, in the character, and in the story that he was willing to walk away from all the money, even when he needed it most.

Rocky won best picture at the Academy Awards in 1977. Stallone and his fellow castmates received Oscar nominations. The film also won for best director and best editing.

"I never would have sold it," Stallone later told the *New York Times*. "I would have hated myself for selling out . . . My wife agreed, and said she'd be willing to move to a trailer in the middle of a swamp if need be."

Daring Disruptors like Stallone go all in. You should be willing to give up everything to achieve your goal. Your goal deserves your absolute attention and effort.

Just ask the freshmen of the US Naval Academy.

The Final Climb

Each spring, the plebes at the US Naval Academy must make a final climb before they successfully complete their first year.

Their "plebes no more" mission: replace a "Dixie cup" hat on top of a twenty-one-foot granite obelisk, known as the Herndon Monument, with an upperclassman's hat. The Herndon Monument pays homage to Commander William Lewis Herndon, who commanded the SS *Central America*, and died during a three-day hurricane, despite his heroic attempts to save the ship, its sailors, and the passengers. The monument is a tribute to Herndon's courage, discipline, and teamwork.

To some, the task might seem simple. But there are no ladders, steps, or nearby trees from which to jump. It's chaotic. It's messy. There's vegetable shortening spread all over the obelisk. The plebes cannot wear shoes. Oh, and cadets are spraying the plebes and the monument with water to make everyone and everything extra slippery.

There's no backup plan. They must rise to the occasion to reach the top.

But the chaos is more organized than it appears. There are no individuals here—only a team of one. It's their greatest challenge, and they have no choice but to solve it. It's a continual climb and fall, a fight to the top. They can change strategies, pivot, and find another way. It's them versus the monument. This is their mission, and they must be all in.

The winning strategy often involves forming a human pyramid and using shirts to scrub off the shortening. Once the pyramid is several layers high, the goal is to propel one team member within reach of the cup. Then, it's a matter of precision, since the hat must land perfectly on top of the monument. Once it does, the mission is completed. The plebes erupt in celebration, as they have conquered Herndon, and the human pyramid falls to the ground. Legend has it that the plebe who reaches the top and successfully places the hat will be first in their class to reach the rank of admiral.

The Herndon Climb is the ultimate test of teamwork. It's one unit working together for a common goal. You're relying on the people to your right and left, and above and below you. You must find a way.

A backup plan means you have convinced yourself that it's okay to give up. Not having one means it's incumbent upon you to achieve. Get fully invested. When you never have a backup plan, you can focus solely on crushing your goals.

How to Crush Your Goals in Five Minutes

Goal setting isn't a novel concept. We've all heard about the idea of having goals. The problem is that too many people stop there. Their goals are more like dreams that last for a while and then disappear. Or they have goals, but they don't know how to achieve them. Or they have goals and think they know how to achieve them, but they don't do anything about it. Or they have goals, take a few steps toward them, then give up.

Let's change that.

Goal setting is about taking proactive steps toward a positive future. When it comes to goal setting, your goals should make you S-N-A-P. They should be: specific, nonnegotiable, actionable, and with purpose.

SPECIFIC. Make your goals specific, and include as many details as possible. Vague goals are harder to attain and visualize. For example, rather than say that you want to get a new job, say that starting Monday, you're going to apply to ten jobs a week for two months.

NONNEGOTIABLE. You must own your goals and be responsible for attaining them. Writing down your goals makes them more tangible, and you should read them daily to stay on course. Accountability for their completion starts and stops with you.

ACTIONABLE. Goals are about taking action, and you need a clear process of how to complete them. It's not enough to have an end goal. Create a road map that you can refer to throughout your journey. Track your progress and incorporate feedback. Here's one strategy: try breaking down your goals into components. Rather than tackle a huge goal at once, get small wins by accomplishing micro tasks that sum to the greater goal. For example, if your goal is to build a new house, focus your mind on completing one room at a time. Small steps can fuel your momentum.

PURPOSE. Goals must have an underlying purpose. It's not enough to want something. Connect that desire with why it's important to you. When you connect a goal with purpose, your goal becomes more than another accomplishment. There's now special meaning attached that is propelling you to win.

Now, let's build on these principles and look at ten simple steps to crush your goals in five minutes.

1. Write down five goals you want to achieve in your life.

These are any goals, large or small. No goal is too large, and don't set your boundaries too small. Don't worry what other people will say or think. This is for you.

Look closely at these goals. This may be the first time you've written them down.

2. Read your list out loud.

One by one, say each goal out loud. Don't be shy when you read them. Say them with purpose.

3. Rephrase each goal with "I will."

It's not enough to write "climb Kilimanjaro." You have to own these goals. They can't be vague or intangible. Rewrite your list so it reads in this format: "I will climb Mount Kilimanjaro."

If you're not used to stating goals this way, it may sound silly or uncomfortable at first.

4. Think about why you want this goal.

Focus on the one goal that is most important to you. The "what" is only part of this exercise. The "why" is more critical for your self-understanding.

List the reasons you want this. I asked you to choose five goals to achieve in your life. You could have chosen anything. Why this one? What does it mean to you? Why is it important in your life?

When you understand concretely why you chose this goal and why you are doing it, you will connect outcome with purpose. Goals aren't just about outcomes; they're about the nexus of outcomes (the results of a goal) and purpose (why we want and need that goal). When you connect these two facets, your goal will become more tangible and meaningful to you. Remind yourself why you need to do this.

5. Work backward from your goal to where you are today.

Our path from where we are today to where we want to be may seem foggy. Thinking backward can help provide clarity. Rather than start with where you are today, start with where you want to be. It's the same strategy that Apple and Amazon employ when they set out to create new products. Rather than start with the technology, they begin with the customer experience and work backward to the technology. They begin with where they want to be, and then reverse engineer.

Imagine you're standing at the peak of Kilimanjaro. Close your eyes and breathe the air. Feel the breeze. Imagine the altitude. What do you see? What do you hear?

Now ask yourself: How did you get here? What did you do?

Work backward. How long did it take to scale? With whom did you climb? How did you travel there?

Work back even further. How did you get time off from work? What time of year did you go? How did you pay for your trip?

And further. How did you prepare? What kind of training did you do?

Work all the way back to the point where you wrote down your goal.

6. Think about a time in your life when you reached a goal.

It can be any goal in your life. It can be riding a bike when you were a child to learning Spanish in high school to running a marathon last year. How did you do it? Was it constant practice? Was it your will and determination? Whatever you did then, I want you to write down how you did it. Next, I want you to write down how it made you feel to accomplish that goal.

Now, I want you to read those answers out loud: the goal, the strategy, and the feeling.

You're going to use the same thought process that produced that earlier result and apply it toward this goal.

7. Work forward to trace your goal back from where you are today.

Now that you've worked backward, connect the dots back to your goal. It's like a rolling pin rolling across dough: for the end product to take shape, after you go back, you must move forward.

The physical motion of retracing your backward movements in a forward trajectory will propel you to act. It will also help you fill in missing steps along the way and refine your action plan.

When you see a clear path on paper in front of you, your goal becomes more achievable. The dots are connected.

8. Be more specific.

Goals that lack specificity are harder to achieve because they're less tangible. Develop your game plan. Add a timeline coupled with a detailed action plan. This is your strategy to get from today to tomorrow to the next day. Without these guideposts, your goals will keep drifting into the future.

Specifics don't mean "I will book a flight by next June."

Instead, your action plan should look like this: "No later than June 5, I will book a flight departing from this city to that city. Since I've already researched flight options, I know that my layover will be in this city, and the cost of this ticket should be no more than this much."

The more details you can specify, the more real this goal becomes. When you can name the cities and dollar amounts, your goal is more tangible. You can feel the airplane ride. You can start brainstorming about how to pay for this adventure.

9. Start with that first step.

Your first step shouldn't be a big one. Ask yourself: What is the simplest, most actionable step I can take right now to work toward achieving my goal?

It can be as simple as printing a map, taping it to your wall, and circling Mount Kilimanjaro. Then draw a line to your hometown. When you see the flight path, it all becomes more real.

10. Take the next step.

Once you have taken that first step, you've crossed the barrier that many people don't. The next step in your action plan becomes much easier once you've taken the initial one. As you implement this routine, ask yourself: Are my goals time bound or timeless? Time-bound goals are goals that you'll achieve by a certain date. Timeless goals have no deadline; you can achieve them anytime. They sound like opposites, but you need both.

You need time-bound goals to create deadlines for achievement. Deadlines instill specificity and discipline. Deadlines make goals more concrete. You also need timeless goals to achieve anytime. However, if timeless goals are too far in the future, they become too remote and less palpable.

Keep taking steps at your own pace. Since you know what your goal looks like forward and backward, getting there is now a matter of one thing: you.

11

IGNORE THE SHORTEST DISTANCE

Sometimes you want success so badly and are willing to do whatever it takes, but you're unsure how to make it happen. You know you're talented, but you can't find that ideal opportunity.

You're twenty-five and still looking for that job.
You're thirty and didn't get that promotion.
You're thirty-five and haven't found the right career.
You're forty and didn't make partner.
You're fifty and haven't started your own business.
You're sixty and feel like you're starting over.
You're seventy and don't have the nest egg you want for retirement.

Timeless goals have replaced your once time-bound goals, and you begin to worry whether you'll ever get your real shot.

As you begin to question everything, an Eternal Excuser tells you that it's always harder than it seems. A Change Chaser then reminds you to take shortcuts—they're everywhere. Then, a Steady Settler whispers that classic principle from the Greek mathematician Archimedes: "The shortest distance between two points is a straight line." Don't overcomplicate, keep it simple, and you'll reach your destination.

Well, what if your path isn't a straight line?

What if your path seems to take longer than everyone else's?

What if it's not so simple for you?

What if things were easier long ago, but more challenging now?

Your life path, your career, and your trajectory aren't always the way you'd like them to be. There are twists and turns. Ups and downs. Starts and stops. And that's okay.

Here's a secret that Lemon Lifers don't like to admit:

> There is no shortest path. It doesn't exist. You can look forever, and you'll never find it. If there were a shortest path, everyone would be on it and be crushing life.

It doesn't matter how old you think you are. You can feel as though you passed all the big birthday milestones, but it's never too late to make it happen. You can make lemonade anytime.

So, if your path isn't a straight line, what do you do?

If you're in this situation, you're among good company with billionaires, celebrities, entrepreneurs, and everyday Daring Disruptors who found their own shortest distance that worked best for them.

And you will, too, if you embrace these seven things:

1. Remember the Art of Lemonadeconomics
2. It's Never Too Late to Find Your Secret Recipe
3. Why Kevin Hart Sells Out Arenas
4. What You Really Want to Do When You Grow Up
5. The Evolution of the Straw
6. Always Walk with a Compass
7. What You, JFK, and Charles de Gaulle All Have in Common

Remember the Art of Lemonadeconomics

Lemonade-ka-what?

Translation: we're going to deconstruct a lemonade stand.

As a child, if you wanted to make money over the summer, you might have opened a lemonade stand—a simple, straightforward plan. Almost everyone loves ice-cold lemonade on a hot summer day.

What's the formula for a successful lemonade stand? There are at least four components:

- Real estate: find the right street corner
- Marketing: have a great sign
- Product: make delicious lemonade
- Customer service: make sure to smile

If you can do these four things, you'll have a successful lemonade stand. You'll make money, feel accomplished, and make others happy. Easy enough. Here's the breakdown of what you may have gained from your childhood lemonade stand:

- Money: high profit margin
- Accomplishment: pride
- Entrepreneurship: built something
- Happiness: spread joy to others

Let's fast-forward to today. You're all grown up. You may have sweet memories of lemonade in your childhood, and decide you want to start a lemonade stand today. If you were to just follow the same traditional four steps—street corner, sign, product, and smile—you probably wouldn't have a successful lemonade stand.

There are several reasons, but the main one is that you're no longer a child. A street corner wouldn't cut it, and real estate wouldn't be free. A cardboard sign wouldn't suffice. Customers would expect freshly baked cookies and fresh-squeezed lemonade. Jumping up and down on the sidewalk likely wouldn't drive customers toward you.

As you can see, it's no longer as simple as following those four steps. Times have changed; you've changed. The lemonade stand represents your life. What made sense during your childhood may not resonate today. So you have to be more innovative and creative. You may need to adapt to a new paradigm. As you adapt, change can feel uncomfortable. How do you maintain continuity? You have a consistent set of values. If the foundation is solid, change won't break it. Sound structures and systems are built not only to withstand change, but also to adapt and grow. If you're building a home, you need a foundation that can withstand all types of weather—and the same applies to your belief system and values. Your foundation must be strengthened to weather life. Not the steady parts, not the happy parts, not the successful parts—all of life.

No matter your path or journey, you should write down the five to ten values that you want to govern your life. The sooner you commit to do this, the better. Keep them in a safe place, so you can refer to your values until you have memorized them. These values will carry you through your successes and failures, your trials and tribulations. When you don't have a foundation or game plan, it's easy to allow chaos to overwhelm you. When you have a list of values and principles to live by, however, the world becomes more orderly. You'll have the lifeboat ready to steer you safely to shore.

Your values will help you adapt in a more organized and thoughtful way. That's why it's imperative that when it's time to make the switch, you can refer to these values that you wrote down during a more peaceful time. Circumstances change, but values don't.

With your values in place, adapting your game plan is an easier endeavor. There's no "perfect" time to flip the switch. Life may get in the way. Time may pass. Opportunities don't seem available. The most important differentiator between Daring Disruptors and everyone else is that Daring Disruptors flip the switch.

It's Never Too Late to Find Your Secret Recipe

Meet Harland.

He held many jobs before he found his calling later in life. Among others, Harland was a streetcar conductor, railroad fireman, insurance salesman, steamboat ferry operator, lighting manufacturer, lawyer, and tire salesman.

Later, he became a chef and operated a motel and restaurant in Kentucky that served customers chicken, country ham, and steaks. At age fifty, Harland finalized a recipe for frying chicken in a pressure fryer that cooked the chicken faster than in a frying pan.

Unfortunately, Harland saw his business crumble when the highway junction in front of his restaurant was relocated. Later, the new interstate highway completely skipped it.

Fearing the worst, he sold his business at a loss and was forced to live on his remaining savings and monthly Social Security check of $105.

Yet in the face of failure, Harland had a plan. If customers couldn't come to him for his fried chicken, he would bring it to them.

Armed with pressure cookers and bags of seasoning, he hit the road. Often sleeping in the back of his car, Harland traveled the country, restaurant by restaurant, to fry his chicken and try to negotiate franchise rights with each restaurant operator. It wasn't until Harland was sixty-two that he franchised his secret recipe for the first time, to Salt Lake City, Utah, restaurant operator Pete Harman.

Over the next twelve years, Harland built a restaurant empire named for his famous chicken, Kentucky Fried Chicken, with more than six hundred locations, before eventually selling the company.

Harland Sanders's path was anything but straight. However, he was a Daring Disruptor who took his own shortest path to find his calling as a chef and entrepreneur who built one of the great quick-service restaurant concepts.

Harland isn't alone. You can be a Daring Disruptor at any age. Take it from these trailblazers who all made it big after age forty.

Vera Wang, one of the world's most talented designers, didn't design her first dress until she was forty.

Samuel L. Jackson has made more than 120 movies, but he didn't get his big break until he was forty-three.

Rodney Dangerfield is one of the funniest comedians of all time, but he didn't gain widespread fame until he appeared on *The Ed Sullivan Show* at age forty-six.

Julia Child wrote her first cookbook at age fifty.

Charles Darwin didn't publish *On the Origin of Species* until he was fifty.

Betty White didn't get her big break until she appeared on *The Mary Tyler Moore Show* when she was fifty-one.

Our culture of instant gratification puts enormous weight on our shoulders. We think that if we don't get accepted to the "right" college, somehow the train gets derailed. We think that if we don't get that fancy internship, our career prospects are doomed. We think that if we don't get into the top law school, our legal career is tarnished. We think that if our first job isn't our dream job, we fell short. We think if we don't "make it" by age thirty, we're toast.

We assume there's this life checklist that must be completed by a certain age. So we create a false sense of urgency that we must figure it all out now. If we don't, somehow we are outcasts who didn't make it.

But life doesn't move at a universal pace. We don't all move together in unison. Your life moves at your pace, on your time. Your parents, friends, classmates, and neighbors all move at their own pace. Some move in a lockstep formation. Others start and stop. Others take winding roads, get lost in the woods, get chased by a bear, call for help, get rescued, get lost again, have their car break down, and then get on their way. The beauty of this dance is that everyone can finish. The dance doesn't have to be graceful or perfect. This isn't musical chairs, where seats are limited. If you want to finish the dance, hustle to learn the moves and finish your dance at your own pace. As long as you're moving, it's okay if it takes longer to get the steps right.

Be sure to recognize the difference, however, between taking longer on your journey as you discover yourself versus discovering yourself up front and not choosing a journey that reflects who you really are. Think back to Career Day, and you'll see why.

In kindergarten, Career Day was simple. You could be anything you wanted: an astronaut, police officer, firefighter, doctor, baseball player. Whatever you wanted to do for your career, all you had to say was, "When I grow up, I'm going to be . . ." It was that simple and straightforward. No hesitation or doubt. For many people, it was the most direct, confident, willful declaration they'll ever make about their career.

In college, a friend told me that he was going to law school, but he didn't want to be a lawyer. Here's how it went down.

"I'm going to law school to be a lawyer. But I don't want to be a lawyer.

"First, I'll work at a big law firm. There, I can learn about mergers and acquisitions. But I don't want to be a corporate lawyer.

"Then, I can get a job at an investment bank, so I can be an investment banker and do big mergers and acquisitions. But I don't want to be an investment banker.

"If I do well in banking, then I can be positioned to get hired at a big private equity firm. Then, I can invest in companies directly, rather than advising them. But I don't want to work in private equity.

"If I do well in private equity, I can get hired at a hedge fund. Then, I can invest in the public markets and make a lot of money. Finally, my dream job."

What?

In business school, a friend told me she was going to work as a consultant. Here's what she said.

"First, I'll work at a big consulting firm. There, I can learn about strategy. But I don't want to be a consultant.

"Then, I can get a job at a consumer products company, so I can be a brand manager. Then I can work on big global brands. But I don't want to be a brand manager.

"If I do well at the consumer products company, then I can get hired at a startup. Then, I can work on a new, innovative product. But I don't want to work at someone else's startup.

"What I really want is to start my own company, and I already have the idea."

What is she waiting for? What are you waiting for? If you know what you want, go get the job you want now. It won't take three different careers to get there.

Your destination may be a lot closer than you realize.

Why Kevin Hart Sells Out Arenas

One moment, you may be inspired.

You may come up with the idea of the century. You stay up all night. You may work feverishly to produce something based on that inspiration. Guess what? The next day, it may go nowhere. The day after that, nowhere. You see where I'm going with this? Inspiration doesn't always lead to the billion-dollar product overnight. It may take days, weeks, months, years of hard work, testing, and refining to get where you want to be. Not everything is an instant hit. There may be periods where you tread water and feel like you're going nowhere.

Many people like to consume inspirational content, whether it's motivational quotes or a good book that get them pumped and ready to conquer the world.

And then they do nothing.

Then they watch a YouTube clip, and they get pumped again.

And then they do nothing.

They keep practicing the same bad habits. They spin their wheels without making any progress.

That ends today. This book is your game plan. It's your platform for action. Take back control of your life and stop pretending how great your life is, how awesome your job is, and how wonderful you feel every day.

Do something about it. No one else will but you.

The trick is to stay motivated and sustain that inspiration, even in moments when you don't feel motivated or excited. You still have to channel that initial spark, passion, and excitement that you had on day one and carry it throughout the highs and lows until you reach your goal.

Change Chasers can't sustain momentum. They want the quick hit, but they're not there for the grind. If they don't hit that jackpot up front, they lose the spark. They need instant gratification. But they check out when the real work begins, when no one wants to invest in their idea, when new prospects won't take their sales calls, when they have to pitch their business over and over again to find new clients. They've headed for the exits before the real work has begun.

The on-demand economy has reduced waiting time to the click of a button. You can order what you want, when you want. In the process, we've become conditioned to demand instant gratification. Whether it's food, movies, TV, clothing, transportation, or dry cleaning, all it takes is one click. If we don't get it now, it's bad customer service. If we don't find immediate meaning in our relationships, they won't work out. If everyone doesn't love you at work on day one, it's time to quit.

Your journey isn't about immediate gratification. Journeys are long and arduous for a reason. Life isn't won and lost on the first day. It took God a week to create heaven and earth. You're not going to do it any faster. If you don't have the patience and tenacity to reach your milestones along the twists and turns in your life, then you're missing the importance of your journey. Your journey is more than an endgame or an ultimate feeling of affirmation. It's an embodiment of your growth and your maturation, a refinement of your purpose, and a redirection of your intentions.

Don't worry about the time it takes to get there. It's all about the work. You can flip on all the switches; you can have the best attitude in the world and try to do the right things. However, if you don't work to make lemonade every day, you'll never be what you aspire to become.

Here's another thing: problems in your way do not and will not magically disappear or resolve themselves. You can't wish for them to go away. Every day you don't solve them means the problem will linger or even grow bigger. Inaction comes at a cost. It's not free. You can't just skip paying your bills and hope that the balance decreases. You can't endlessly complain about your negative work environment and expect the company culture to change. It's up to you to tackle these problems. It's your turn to act. Right the wrongs. Change your circumstances. What are you waiting for? You don't need anyone's permission or sign-off. This isn't third grade. This is your life.

Kevin Hart doesn't sell out arenas around the world because he just got funny one day. Oprah didn't randomly become a billionaire entrepreneur and beloved media megastar. Dwayne Johnson didn't suddenly become one of the biggest movie stars of all time. Magic Johnson wasn't born the greatest point guard in history. Jeff Bezos didn't change the world of retail because he came up with a powerful idea. Every one of these people hustled to get where they are today.

Nothing will be handed to you. Yes, you may get lucky, but luck isn't a strategy. You have to want it more than everyone else. You have to work to get where you want to go. It's easy to forget about Steve Jobs working out of a garage or Jeff Bezos using a door for a desk or Tyler Perry sleeping in his car. They've all made it, so it's easy to forget how long their road was. But they, too, toiled down a long path to build their reality.

So you can plan, strategize, position, debate, analyze, and ponder. At the end of the day, the only thing that counts is whether you make lemonade. You have to execute. What's your output? That's what the world sees. There are other things that matter on the inside for you, like your effort, values, and work ethic. Those are important to you and can help provide internal feedback. But others see your impact. Don't confuse the two. When you're working on yourself, the journey matters and can help you become better as you navigate life. When you're working to build a business or your career, it's the finished product that matters. You're judged for your output and impact.

How do you get there?

It doesn't matter how many steps you take back. It matters how many steps you take forward. Ask yourself: Am I moving, or am I stagnant? That's the first choice you make. If you're stagnant and on the sideline, you're out of the game. You're already finished. If you're moving, you're one step closer to where you want to be. You may be moving in the wrong direction, or you may need to move faster. That you can adjust. You can shuffle priorities and change your strategy. But don't be hard on yourself if you don't find your dream job on day one. That's the trap of instant gratification.

Too many people give up before they've reached their destination. Or they're shouting from the stands, not playing on the field. Step one is get on the field. It's where all the action takes place. When you're in the game, you can see more opportunities.

Many people get down on themselves if they don't make 100 percent gains. They expect everything to click in the first week or first month. When it doesn't, they think they failed and want to quit. It's good to swing for the fences, but don't fall into the trap of becoming a Change Chaser. No one will fault you for striving for smaller, daily wins.

If you take one step toward your goal, you're one step closer to greatness than every Eternal Excuser.

Steady Settlers get trapped in a mind-set that if they don't get hired by the best law firm out of law school and don't make partner in ten years, then they fell short.

They're thinking about it all wrong. It's not the big leaps that define you.

One hundred days of 1 percent wins takes you to the same place as one day with a 100 percent win.

Get there on your own terms, even when others don't see your path.

What You Really Want to Do When You Grow Up

The interview starts unassumingly, and then the interviewer proceeds to ask a slew of questions:

"How many golf balls can fit inside a 747?"

"How many stops signs are there in America?"

"Can you sell me this pen?"

Then the interview takes a sharp left turn, and the interviewer throws out this question:

"What do you really want to do when you grow up?"

If you've heard that line before, you're not alone.

"So, Frank, thanks for coming in. I reviewed your résumé, but wow, quite a few jobs here. Good companies, but three different jobs in ten years? One job in marketing. One job in sales. One job in operations. What do you really want to do when you grow up?"

That ubiquitous line has made the rounds on the interview circuit from New York to London to Sydney and back again. It's usually thrown at a prospective hire by a recruiter or manager as somewhat of a dig for having worked in several different jobs or industries. Often, it's asked in a condescending tone and accompanied by a laugh or smirk.

The suggestion is that you bounce around from job to job without clear focus. There's an underlying assumption that your decision to not have one job at the same company for a prolonged period makes you somehow less reliable or unsure of your path.

Let's break down the question in two parts to further understand its absurdity.

"WHAT DO YOU REALLY WANT TO DO . . ." The first half of the question suggests that your career choices to date haven't been serious. The intimation is that whatever you have done in the past was somehow pretend or a joke (notice the emphasis on the "really").

". . . WHEN YOU GROW UP?" As if your "poor" career choices weren't enough, now you're immature. Apparently, you aren't old enough or wise enough to think independently or make viable decisions.

Of course, the question is total nonsense. It's traditionally asked by an Eternal Excuser or Steady Settler who can't possibly understand the rationale or context of other people's decision-making if those decisions differ from their own. A more logical and useful question would be to ask you why you made a certain career choice and what you learned from the experience.

There is a societal tendency to put people in boxes based on their pedigree, primarily their schooling and employers. Too little room is given for explanation or context. Too little room is given for exploration and experimentation. People's lives get reduced to an 8½" x 11" piece of paper, where they're expected to explain their life choices. For some, this method is an efficient way to review credentials. The problem is that it misses what's truly important—the journey. What you learned along the way while you're finding your way is more important than where you worked or how long you worked there.

If you find your calling in life when you're seven years old, and you know you want to be a firefighter, then the decision is easy for you. If you know when you're a college freshman that medicine is the field for you, then you have a clear path to realize your dream.

Everyone else has probably heard a mouthful from their parents, sisters, brothers, grandparents, in-laws, friends, and everyone else as to why they should enter this field or take that job.

"If you want to be a millionaire, go work on Wall Street."

"If you want to be a billionaire, go work in Silicon Valley."

"If you're smart and good at science, go be a doctor."

"If you're smart and not good at science, go be a lawyer."

These advice givers know one thing and one thing only: what worked for them. Not you, them. They may have perspective and experience, and the wrinkles and gray hair to prove it. Yet they don't know what your passion is or where your heart lies.

So when you hear the question "What do you really want to do when you grow up?" the easy answer is "Never work for you." Then, think of Frank. People will make assumptions about you your whole life. The reality is that Frank learned more in those three jobs than he would have had he spent those ten years in any one of those jobs. Frank now has worked in sales, marketing, and operations, which arguably makes him a stronger asset because he has experienced multiple aspects of a business and understands how they connect. He knows what he likes and doesn't like. He wasn't afraid to jump in and find the best fit.

Sometimes, the shortest distance is the easy choice. It's the lazy option. It's the one that doesn't allow you to break the mold and find the right path for you. Don't be afraid if finding your calling takes longer. Some people find their calling at age seven or seventeen. Some find it at twenty-seven, thirty-seven, or forty-seven. You won't know unless you follow the Five Es:

The Five Es

Explore	The more opportunities you explore, the more opportunities you can create.
Endeavor	Your journey may not be the shortest distance. When you endeavor, you focus on your own unique journey.
Experiment	Keep experimenting to find the right formula, the right solution, and the right choice for you.
Embrace	Embrace opportunities, people, and obstacles to get from your starting point to your endpoint.
Engage	Engage in everything you do with full stamina and dedication.

When you do these five things, you're in the game. You're moving, and on your way to finding your calling and getting fully invested. During that journey, every experience is an opportunity to collect another tool for your toolbox.

As that toolbox fills, you'll have the wisdom and confidence to know not to work with someone who asks what you really want to do when you grow up. The answer to that question will be simple: you've been doing it, you are doing it, and you'll keep doing it.

Even if it takes you more time, I want you to remember two things: progress takes time, and when it happens, it can happen rapidly.

The Evolution of the Straw

Over the past five thousand years, there have been two primary changes to the classic straw. One man made it sturdier. The other made it more flexible. There have been other variations over the years (including the modern reusable straw), but these are arguably the two most significant advancements. When we think of technological innovation over the span of five thousand years, we envision revolutionary advancements that made life better for each generation. Yet the straw has experienced little change over several millennia.

The first straws can be traced to 3000 BC and were made by the Sumerians. The first known straw, which was recovered in a Sumerian tomb and likely used to drink beer, was a gold tube decorated with lapis lazuli, a blue precious stone.

CHANGE #1: It wasn't until the nineteenth century that the first major change happened. While relaxing with a mint julep in his Washington, DC, home, Marvin Chester Stone noticed that his rye grass straw, the straw of choice at the time, was virtually dissolved in his drink. Although the resulting residue at the bottom of his glass was a normal occurrence, Stone didn't enjoy the grassy taste that mixed with his bourbon. Stone experimented with an alternative straw made of paper, which led him to invent a machine that produced manila paper straws. By adding a paraffin wax coat, Stone prevented the straw from dissolving in a drink. By 1888, the modern straw was born.

CHANGE #2: The second major milestone in the evolution of the straw occurred in the 1930s, at Varsity Sweet Shop, a soda fountain parlor in San Francisco. Joseph B. Friedman, the brother of the shop's owner, saw his young daughter, Judith, struggling to drink her milkshake from a paper straw while seated at the counter. Inspired to help solve her dilemma, he inserted a screw into the top portion of a paper straw and used dental floss to wrap the paper into the screw threads. When he removed the screw, the straw became flexible. By 1937, the bendable straw was born.

Five thousand years of straws, and the two most significant changes occurred within fifty years of each other. Both inventors substantially increased the practical utility of the product, but neither Stone nor Friedman invented the first straw. Rather, they built upon existing infrastructure by making small, yet impactful changes.

The simplest tweaks can yield the biggest benefits. Sometimes, it may feel that you're not on the right path. You feel as though you're treading water, stuck in a maze, lost. Before you make a massive overhaul, remember the evolution of the straw. Change takes time. There can be periods with no or little progress, followed by periods of rapid advancement. You may already be on your shortest path and not even realize it. You may just need to tweak your direction, switch your sail, or change your rhythm.

Like the evolution of the straw, certain times will require you to be durable, while others will demand flexibility. You need to be durable enough to withstand the obstacles along your path, but flexible enough to follow your path when it isn't a straight line.

When you get there—and you will—take time to enjoy a milkshake or sip a mint julep.

Always Walk with a Compass

Durability and flexibility are essential to your success, but we're also creatures of habit and routine. It's easy to get stuck performing the same tasks day in and day out. Soon, days, weeks, and even months have passed without much notice. Where has the time gone?

We wake up, go to work, work, go home, sleep, and do it all over again. It's a continuous cycle. Routines are helpful, and automation is more efficient, but you shouldn't live on autopilot. You'll miss the wonderful detours, opportunities, and spontaneity that make life most fulfilling. How do you break that cycle and take a hard look at your daily routine, to evaluate whether you're living your best life?

The best advice I received for my wedding was this: Take a moment during the night to take your bride's hand and leave the ballroom together. Then look back inside and take in the moment. It's an entirely different perspective when you step away from the action and you're on the outside looking in. It's important to be in the action, but it's equally important to be able to pause, step away, and take it all in.

It's the same when you're walking in a park or even down the street. The next time you go for a walk, bring a compass. You don't need a real one. This is a mental compass. Take note of the way you walk. Do you walk quickly or slowly? Are you in a trance? Do you look down? Do you make eye contact? Do you walk with purpose?

The compass represents the four directions in your life, and you might not be leveraging the full power they provide. Most people focus straight ahead. They think it's the shortest distance. So, they blindly follow what's in front of them. Straight to work. Straight home. Straight to the gym. Straight home. Straight to the store. Straight home. Straight to bed. The cycle repeats. Straight ahead is where the action seems to take place.

If you're only looking straight ahead when you walk, you're missing the fuller picture. How often do you look left and right when you're not crossing the street? How often do you look up, or behind you? When you look in all directions, you're more informed about how best to move forward.

The four directions of your mental compass are different from an actual compass: front, back, up, and down.

Front. The front is where you're headed. This is the wide, open road and blank canvas of your life. The front is a 180-degree angle that includes left, right, and straight. It includes your peripheral vision, not just what is directly in front of you.

It's up to you the path you'll take, and how you'll get there.

Back. The back is where you've been. It's your triumphs and failures. It's the good and bad.

It's up to you how you channel them in your journey.

Up. Up is where those you admire have come before you. You look up to them. You emulate them. They are your mentors and teachers.

It's up to you how and what you learn from them.

Down. Down is where your doubters live. These are the naysayers, the disbelievers. They don't want you to move forward. They relish your failure.

It's up to you the role they play in your life.

The next time you walk, think of all four directions. Straight ahead is not where all the action takes place. You can't understand what's in front of you unless you understand the interconnectivity of the other three directions.

When you understand what's behind you, you know where you've come from, and what it took to get here.

When you understand what's above you, you have people to emulate and goals to accomplish.

When you understand what's beneath you, you have the doubters to remind you of your greatness.

Remember this the next time you walk your walk, even if it's at an airport. An airport can teach you more about your life path than just about anything else. What you'll find is that your journey may not be as twisted or delayed as it seems. Your travels may not be as long as they appear. Your path may not be as much of an outlier as you once thought.

What You, JFK, and Charles de Gaulle All Have in Common

It's not every day that you get compared to JFK or Charles de Gaulle.

Or, in this case, the airports that bear their names.

The next time you pass through JFK in New York City, Charles de Gaulle in Paris, or your local airport, recall that the secret to understanding your unique life path can be found inside an airport. There, you'll find the hard truths about your journey.

Flights leave without you. If you're late to the gate, your flight may have departed. If you don't show up, the party starts without you. Don't expect people to wait for you.

Flights get delayed. Bad weather. Mechanical issues. Not everything starts on time. They may not be ready for you. You may not be ready for them.

Flights get canceled. People change their minds. People will cancel on you. Opportunities have expiration dates. The unexpected does and will happen.

Traffic to the airport. Holiday weekend. Construction. It's rarely smooth sailing on the way. Some are blocking you or are in your way. Find a way around them.

You get upgraded. The exit row. The last seat in business class. The row to yourself on a long-haul flight. Sometimes, you're lucky.

You get the middle seat. Congrats—it's just the three of us for the next fourteen hours. Sometimes, you're unlucky.

Your luggage doesn't fit. The compartment is too small. Your luggage is too big. There's no more room. Sometimes, it's not the right fit, no matter how hard you try.

Time to kill. Sometimes you're early for your flight. You've read every magazine, browsed every store, and scouted every food option. You won't lose points for showing up early and prepared.

Time is against you. Sometimes, you're just late. You're running through the terminal. You can't find your way. But when you read the signs and ask for help, you get there.

The security line is long. The line goes on for miles. Sometimes, you have to wait your turn. Or find another way through.

The security line is short. No one showed up but you.

The flight is bumpy. All turbulence. It happens.

The flight is smooth. No turbulence. It happens.

The food court is closed. You showed up, but they didn't. Your expectations and their expectations may not match. Right place, wrong time.

There is no food court. You're hungry and ready, but the good food court is in the other terminal. Wrong place, right time.

Your luggage came out first. The conveyor belt starts, and there's your bag. Sometimes, you do everything right, and good things happen.

They lost your luggage. The conveyor belt starts, and your bag is nowhere to be found. Sometimes, you do everything right, but bad things happen anyway.

Departures can be exciting. That vacation to Mexico.

Departures can be disappointing. The return flight from that vacation to Mexico.

Departures can be annoying. The last-minute, one-day work trip.

Departures can be scary. Saying goodbye to your loved ones.

Arrivals can be exciting. Welcome home. Your family and friends are waiting with balloons and hugs.

Arrivals can be disappointing. Welcome home. It's just you.

Arrivals can be annoying. You can't remember where you parked your car.

Arrivals can be scary. Everything seems unfamiliar when you step off the plane.

Sometimes, you're at gate 47, and your flight gets moved to gate 1. The shortest distance doesn't always mean to run forty-six gates to your destination. Sometimes, you have to go down corridors and other terminals before you get to your final destination. Other times, there's a shuttle at gate 45 that takes you right there.

Somehow, despite all the ups and downs of travel, the delays and cancellations, the bumpy rides and the lost luggage, people still get to where they need to go. It may be later than expected. It may be a frustrating trip. You may not want to do it again. But eventually, you get there. You reach your destination. You may have been knocked, lost your cool, been told no, not been helped, or been treated disrespectfully.

Whether your flight is nonstop or has three layovers, a train, and a bus, we all find a way to get there in the end. Life is like that too. It's all about your perspective and how you choose to experience your journey. You'll find a way from A to B. Despite how you may feel at one time, your last flight is not really your last flight. No matter how terrible or how enthralling the last flight, there are more trips to take, more sights to see, more experiences to be had, more adventures to enjoy. You're better prepared than you realize.

Switch On: Motion

We each have our own shortest distance that we need to figure out to reach our goals. Find *your* shortest distance. Not what Steady Settlers or "society" or your friends or family tell you is the shortest distance, because that one rarely works. Often, you experience unique and personal twists and turns along the way. For example, you got a late start, or you took longer to reach your destination. Daring Disruptors understand this, and that's why they find their own shortest distance.

The longer path can sometimes lead to breakthrough discoveries, and Daring Disruptors are comfortable with venturing off the shortest path to see where things might take them. If your path is different from someone else's, you can still reach the same destination—on your terms. You might find that you finish ahead, even if you cross the finish line behind.

The path to the other side is often neither straight nor simple. That deters many from even trying. So they give up too soon.

For those willing to invest the time and energy, remember this: after the struggle, there's greatness on the other side.

So many dreams at first seem impossible. And then they seem improbable. And then when we summon the will, they soon become inevitable.

—Christopher Reeve

CONCLUSION:
LEAD THE LEMONADE LIFE

Lead the life you want to live

Everyone is searching for happiness and meaning in their lives. You're not alone in your journey.

How does an Eternal Excuser find happiness? From complaining and criticism. *Happiness is the art of the complaint.*

How does a Steady Settler find happiness? From a résumé and perceived security. *Happiness is the art of keeping up appearances.*

How does a Change Chaser find happiness? From jumping on the next bandwagon. *Happiness is the art of the chase.*

A Daring Disruptor, however, doesn't need these external things to achieve happiness. Happiness and fulfillment come from within.

Remember—your greatest happiness is already inside. You can achieve whatever you want, whenever you want, when you let your happiness out. Your ability to create, achieve, love, strive, risk, and dare is what drives your happiness. They say you get wiser as you get older. I don't want you to wait until you're older. I want you to get wiser now. Start making these changes today. Start flipping these switches.

Only you can flip the five switches that will change your life.

When you do, you'll escape the Lemon Life and start leading the Lemonade Life.

The Five Switches That Will Change Your Life

P = Perspective

R = Risk

I = Independence

S = Self-Awareness

M = Motion

Switch #1: P Is for Perspective

Change your perspective to change your possibilities.

Your new mind-set will help open a pathway to your transformation. Your expanded perspective will redefine your worldview and will reshape what's possible in your life. It all starts with perspective, and your positive mind-set is your solid foundation.

Switch #2: R Is for Risk

Understand the rewards of risk to make better decisions.

Your new ability to remove internal roadblocks will clear the path to develop your edge. Now that you approach life through the dual lenses of risk and reward, you'll have a clearer understanding of what's at stake.

Switch #3: I Is for Independence

Avoid the herd mentality to gain freedom of choice.

The sooner you escape the herd mentality, the sooner you can make the decisions that are uniquely right for you. The herd mentality is about them. Your life is about you. You no longer need the comfort of the herd. Your independent mind will make you more daring and bolder. You're not afraid to be wrong or go against the grain. Independence is your pathway to freedom, and now you set your own pace, on your own path, on your own terms.

Switch #4: S Is for Self-Awareness

Master yourself to master your life.

Your heightened self-awareness will connect you more deeply to the person you really are and the person you want to become. The better you understand yourself, the better equipped you are to understand how you'll navigate life and conquer the world. Now you see things you *need* to see, not necessarily what you *want* to see. You hear things you *need* to hear, not necessarily what you *want* to hear.

Switch #5: M Is for Motion

Make lemonade to change your circumstances.

You can achieve success with the abilities and tools you already have. However, tools are powerless without action. This is your time to shine, and only you control your spotlight. Find your own path, make lemonade, and go all in. Keep moving. No one is going to do this for you, except you.

Ah, the Glory Days

Think about a time in your life that you cherish. Think about a time in your life when all felt peaceful. Life was easy. Your glory days. All of us have that memory. Is that memory from when you were a child? Is it from school or college? Is it from five years ago?

Parents and grandparents love to reminisce about the glory days.

"When I was your age, we used to . . . Those were the days."

What feelings do those memories evoke? I bet they bring you to a happy place. I bet they inspire you. I bet all felt right with the world. When you think about your life today, what do you see? Are you living your glory days now? That's not a trick question, and you don't have to choose among memories. You can have multiple periods of glory days, when all felt peaceful and life was easier. Whatever happy feelings you have, I want you to connect them to your life today.

Glory days don't have to be a temporary state or distant memory, which is how most people refer to them.

Eternal Excusers are the first to say, "Well, times are different now."

By some standards, that's true. You may no longer get a summer vacation like when you were a child. The economy may have changed. The neighborhood may have been redeveloped.

Steady Settlers are next to say, "The glory days were high school."

Lots of free time. No real responsibilities. "I broke my school's all-time passing record, and we went undefeated."

Change Chasers chime in, "Glow-in-the-dark bracelet investment in the 1980s."

We can list a million excuses why the glory days can be no longer. Life is more complicated now. Things are done differently. It's not as easy as it used to be.

Now, imagine if you ask the CEO of a company how his or her business is doing today versus twenty years ago, and these are the responses:

"There's more competition abroad now, and they undercut our prices."

"Our technology didn't keep up with the times."

"Real estate is too expensive, so we had to close locations."

"We don't have a true social media strategy. We didn't need one in those days."

"Consumer preferences have changed."

What would you say to this CEO? First, would you buy a product or service from a company like this? Second, do you have any confidence in this CEO? Third, you would ask how this company is going to adapt. Your environment will change. The times will change. You will change. It's how you adapt and respond that matters.

Your glory days don't need to be frozen in your past. If you're still thinking back to the time that you made history, you're a Steady Settler. You'll get eaten alive, every time, by someone hungrier. Do you really want to be a Steady Settler, sitting on a porch, telling people about the good old days? Do you want to be an Eternal Excuser, complaining how the glory days are gone forever? Or do you want to still be living your glory days today?

Grab every rebound off the backboard as if you h
Shoot every free throw as if the college scout were w
you're trying out for the high school track team. Cor
opponent of hustle. Use the wisdom of a veteran to hu
this your freshman year, not your victory tour.

Your glory days don't have to be that one, shining

What are you going to do *now* to reinvent yoursel

What are you going to do *today* to adapt?

What are you going to do *tomorrow* to ensure that
days? Not *those* glory days, but your *new* glory days.

Your glory days of today—and tomorrow.

When You Reach the Sum

The Lemonade Life isn't a destination.

Getting there is the first step. The Lemonade Life
to create your best self and reach your full potential, eve
of you is not your best friend, your older sibling, or y
star. You can incorporate elements of other people, but
will always be you.

Daring Disruptors don't reach the Lemonade Life
Daring Disruptors, it's not about reaching the Lemonad
ing it. It's the beginning pathway to lead a fuller life.

You can learn something from anyone—even L
Chasers lack substance, but we can appreciate their "sl
look (even if they're cavalier). Eternal Excusers compl
risk aversion may save them from significant loss (even
potential). Steady Settlers may be stuck in a familiar rut
their focus on stability (even if they're defined by oth
success). So while you lead the Lemonade Life and leave
never pass up an opportunity to learn, think, and grow.

On May 29, 1953, at 11:30 a.m., Edmund H

aineer Tenzing Norgay became the first climbers confirmed to reach
nmit of Mount Everest.

Steady Settler thinks that once you conquer Everest, you've reached the
le. Not so. After conquering Everest, Hillary reached the South Pole by
, tackled a 1,500-mile motorboat trek up the Ganges River, and traveled
North Pole with astronaut Neil Armstrong.

aring Disruptors don't reach the mountaintop and call it quits.

ey keep climbing.

ey keep daring.

ey keep reaching peaks.

is is your new way of life.

hen you reach the summit, find your next one.

d always find time for a cold glass of lemonade.

DISCUSSION QUESTIONS

1. What does the Lemonade Life mean to you? How can you apply its principles to your life, work, relationships, and outlook?

2. Which of the five switches resonated most with you?

   P Is for Perspective: *Change your perspective to change your possibilities.*
   R Is for Risk: *Understand the rewards of risk to make better decisions.*
   I Is for Independence: *Avoid the herd mentality to gain freedom of choice.*
   S Is for Self-Awareness: *Master yourself to master your life.*
   M Is for Motion: *Make lemonade to change your circumstances.*

3. Why do you think Daring Disruptors flourish? How can you apply the characteristics of Daring Disruptors to your own life, at home and at work?

4. The Lemonade Life is about leading life on your own terms, with purpose and possibility. What does it mean to you to create purpose and possibility in your life?

5. Do you believe that success leads to happiness, or that happiness leads to success? Can both be true?

6. What's your favorite morning routine? If you don't have a morning routine, are you more willing to adopt one after reading this book? Which one would you choose?

7. Have you experienced a Jerk Pyramid at work? What did it do to morale and culture at your organization? If the senior leadership team

didn't address the situation, what proactive steps did you take or could you have taken?

8. Have you met Mike Millionaire before? Why do you think people keep up with the Joneses? What do you think is the most effective method to stop keeping up with the Joneses?

9. Does your team at work have the freedom to put up their hand and put down their foot? Do your organization's leaders encourage original ideas and probing questions? If not, what can you do to create a more open atmosphere?

10. What do you think is the biggest misconception about entrepreneurship? What do you think Lemonade Lifers understand about risk and independence that Lemon Lifers don't?

11. Why do you think Lemon Lifers ultimately don't find their best self? What is it about Lemonade Lifers that enables them to lead a life complete with purpose and possibility?

12. Have you ever found yourself living in the Chasm of Can't? How did it affect your work and home life? What are the biggest roadblocks that have held you back? What do you think is the best strategy to break free?

13. When is the last time you cultivated your wolfpack? What types of people do you want to bring into your wolfpack?

14. Patterns play a critical role in our lives. How have you used the power of patterns to further your own life goals?

15. This book discusses several simple ways you can create happiness in your life. Which are your favorites, and if you could pick one to add to your daily life, which one would you choose?

16. What are your seven wonders of the world? How can having a gratitude journal help you boost happiness each morning?

17. If you could have a give-get relationship with yourself, what are some things you could give up in order to get?

18. This book stresses the importance of having a life purpose and understanding the why behind the what. Why do you think it's critical to have an underlying mission? What's your life purpose?

19. As we learned with the evolution of the straw, change can take time. What do you think are the most important elements of change management? What role can technology play? How can leaders inspire to create buy-in from employees, customers, shareholders, and other stakeholders?

20. What is one positive habit or behavior you learned from the book that you plan to incorporate into your daily life? What proactive steps will you take to ensure that it becomes part of your regular routine?

21. How can you apply the 5X Rule at work and at home?

22. Why is it so important to take it personally and always take no for an answer? Can you think of a time in your life at work when you practiced these principles and it helped you? How will you apply these principles going forward?

ACKNOWLEDGMENTS

Thank you, thank you, thank you.

My heart is filled with gratitude.

First and foremost, thank you for reading my book. There are many things you could be doing right now, and I'm grateful that you chose to dedicate your time to this. I hope this book inspires you to find more happiness, more greatness, and more success in your life.

This book has my name on the front cover, but many talented people behind the scenes made this book possible, and I'm grateful to each of you.

To my literary agent, Jill Marsal, thank you for the straight talk, honest feedback, and great insights. Go Torreys!

Thank you to my wonderful partners at HarperCollins. Brian Hampton and Jeff James, thank you for sharing my vision for *The Lemonade Life* and for believing in me. To the entire HarperCollins Leadership team, especially Hiram Centeno, Sicily Axton, Kathie Johnson, and many others, thank you for your friendship, energy, passion, and commitment to lead the Lemonade Life.

To my talented editors, Tim Burgard and Amanda Bauch, thank you for your tireless work and patience to make this book what it is today. Thank you for your guidance, discipline, sharp focus, and positivity.

To Belinda Bass, thank you for your eye-catching cover design. And to Mallory Collins, thank you for your beautiful interior design.

Thank you to the entire team and all our partners at Make Lemonade, for inspiring people to lead a better financial life. Thanks for your endless commitment to make personal finance simpler. And to those we serve, thank you for all your support, and I hope we're making your life better every day.

Thank you to the amazing professionals at *Forbes*, especially Randall Lane, Janet Novack, Halah Touryalai, Kristin Stoller, Kelly Erb, Jon Ponciano, and the entire *Forbes* team. It's an honor to work with all of you.

Thank you, Libby Kane and the incredible team at *Business Insider*.

To my friends and family, thank you for all the love. Thank you to my parents, Stuart and Judy Friedman, for instilling in me the importance of reading and writing, and for raising me right. To my brother, Josh, for his humor and lifelong friendship. To my in-laws, Larry and Barb King, for your support, and to Danny King, for being my other little brother. To my wonderful grandparents, I know you're smiling.

I have been blessed with many genuine friendships over the years. To all my friends, you have inspired and encouraged me since childhood. From Beverly to Harvard to Wharton, and all before and in between, thank you sincerely for your friendship. You all know who you are. I've learned so much from each of you.

Thank you to the all-star team at CNN and HLN. Special thanks to Scott Warren, David Siff, Selin Darkalstanian, Wendy Vinglinsky, and the entire *MichaeLA* team. Michaela Pereira, you are genuine, authentic, compassionate, and an amazing talent.

Thank you to the team at the Harry Walker Agency, my speakers' bureau, for all your support.

To my wife, Sarah, thank you for being my best friend and my inspiration. You're patient, supportive, and kind like no other. You're a positive force for good in the world. I'm so blessed that you're my wife. Thank you for your grace. I love you. Thank you to Charlie and Drew, the sunshine of my life, for making every day brighter. You spread happiness wherever you are, especially at home. I'm so fortunate to be your dad, and I love you.

From elementary school through business school, I have been fortunate to learn from some of the greatest teachers. Thank you to all our teachers for everything you do every day, and for instilling within me a passion for learning. Thank you especially to Ira Moskow, Jill Cunningham, Mike Bartkoski, Bill Hiatt, Chuck Kloes, Ed Mandel, Joe Cooper, Joel Grossman, Milton

Cummings Jr., and so many others. To the late Gil Chesterton, my high school newspaper advisor, thank you for the opportunity.

Thank you to David Gergen—your leadership class at Harvard continues to inspire me, and your words of wisdom have stayed with me all these years. Michael Waldman, your speechwriting class at Harvard helped hone my writing. To the late Ted Sorensen, thank you for sharing your gift of storytelling and writing (and for the JFK stories).

Thank you, Peter Malkin, for your friendship, mentorship, and generous spirit.

Thank you, Monsignor Robert T. Ritchie, the rector at St. Patrick's Cathedral, for your wisdom and guidance.

There are so many authors who write with authenticity and purpose. I admire your work and impact, and especially thank Simon Sinek, Brené Brown, Gretchen Rubin, Dan Pink, Kim Scott, Gary Vaynerchuk, Seth Godin, Adam Grant, Susan Cain, Malcolm Gladwell, Shawn Achor, and Marshall Goldsmith.

Thank you to everyone who has ever told me no—it didn't work.

Thank you for spreading the message of *The Lemonade Life* to readers around the world. There's more happiness in the world because of you.

For those who share this book with a loved one, friend, or colleague who you think can be inspired, thank you. I look forward to the many new friendships from around the world that are yet to come.

New York
March 2019

NOTES

INTRODUCTION

xv In 2016: Robert W. Wood, "Lunch with Warren Buffett Cost $3.45M, but You Can Write It Off on Your Taxes," *Forbes*, June 11, 2016, https://www.forbes .com/sites/robertwood/2016/06/11/lunch-with-warren-buffett-costs-3-45m-but -you-can-write-it-off-on-your-taxes.

xvi six-year-old: Patricia Sellers, "Warren Buffett's Secret to Staying Young: 'I Eat Like a Six-Year-Old,'" *Fortune*, May 12, 2017, http://fortune.com/2015/02/25 /warren-buffett-diet-coke/.

xvi principles that have guided: Benjamin Graham and David L. Dodd, *Security Analysis*, 6th ed. (New York: McGraw-Hill Education, 2008), xi–xii.

xvi same house since 1958: Nathaniel Lee, "Warren Buffett Lives in a Modest House That's Worth .001% of His Total Wealth—Here's What It Looks Like," *Business Insider*, December 4, 2017, http://www.businessinsider.com/warren -buffett-modest-home-bought-31500-looks-2017-6.

CHAPTER 2: MEET THE LEMON LIFERS

15 how many millionaires, billionaires: Abigail Hess, "10 Ultra-Successful Millionaire and Billionaire College Dropouts," CNBC, May 10, 2017, https://www .cnbc.com/2017/05/10/10-ultra-successful-millionaire-and-billionaire-college -dropouts.html.

18 plan "not to lose": Daniel Kahneman and Amos Tversky, "Choices, Values, and Frames," *American Psychologist* 39, no. 4 (January 1984): 341–50, http://dx .doi.org/10.1037/0003-066X.39.4.341.

21 FOMO: Dan Herman, "Introducing Short-Term Brands: A New Branding Tool for a New Consumer Reality," *Journal of Brand Management* 7, no. 5 (2000): 330–40: http://doi:10.1057/bm.2000.23; and *The Harbus*, "Social Theory at HBS: McGinnis' Two FOs," May 10, 2014, http://www.harbus.org /2004/social-theory-at-hbs-2749/.

CHAPTER 3: WHEN LIFE GIVES YOU LEMONS

26 **Eat a live frog:** "Eat a Live Frog Every Morning, and Nothing Worse Will Happen to You the Rest of the Day," Quote Investigator, April 3, 2013, https://quote investigator.com/2013/04/03/eat-frog/.

27 **save your frog for later in the day:** Francesca Gino and Bradley Staats, "Your Desire to Get Things Done Can Undermine Your Effectiveness," *Harvard Business Review*, March 22, 2016, https://hbr.org/2016/03/your-desire-to-get -things-done-can-undermine-your-effectiveness.

27 **Ben Franklin's favorite morning routine:** Kevan Lee, "The Morning Routines of the Most Successful People," *Fast Company*, July 30, 2014, https://www.fast company.com/3033652/the-morning-routines-of-the-most-successful-people.

27 **What good shall I do this day?:** Lee, "Morning Routines."

27 *ikigai*: Toshimasa Sone et al., "Sense of Life Worth Living (*Ikigai*) and Mortality in Japan: Ohsaki Study," *Psychosomatic Medicine* 70, no. 6 (2008):709–15, https://doi: 10.1097/PSY.0b013e31817e7e64.

28 **Researchers at the University of North Carolina:** Karen M. Grewen et al., "Warm Partner Contact Is Related to Lower Cardiovascular Reactivity," *Behavioral Medicine* 29, no. 3 (2003): 123–30, https://doi.org/10.1080 /08964280309596065; Harland Sanders, *Col. Harland Sanders: The Autobiography of the Original Celebrity Chef* (KFC Corporation: Louisville, 2012).

28 **Researchers have found that journaling:** Robert A. Emmons and Michael E. McCullough, "Counting Blessings Versus Burdens: An Experimental Investigation of Gratitude and Subjective Well-Being in Daily Life," *Journal of Personality and Social Psychology* 84, no. 2 (2003): 377–89, https://greatergood .berkeley.edu/images/application_uploads/Emmons-CountingBlessings.pdf.

28 **maximize the benefits of gratitude:** Jessica Stillman, "You Can Supercharge Your Happiness with This Simple Gratitude Practice, Science Says," *Inc.com*, April 6, 2017, https://www.inc.com/jessica-stillman/you-can -supercharge-your-happiness-with-this-simple-gratitude-practice-science-s.html.

28 **writing quality matters less than your sincerity:** Betsy Mikel, "The Best-Kept Secret to Writing Short, Meaningful Thank-You Notes," *Inc.com*, July 27, 2018, https://www.inc.com/betsy-mikel/do-you-really-need-to-send-a-thank-you-note -heres-what-science-has-to-say.html.

28 **research from the University of Chicago:** Amit Kumar and Nicholas Epley, "Undervaluing Gratitude: Expressers Misunderstand the Consequences of Showing Appreciation," *Psychological Science* 29, no. 9 (September 1, 2018): 1423–35, https://doi.org/10.1177/0956797618772506.

28 **separate research study:** Brenda H. O'Connell, Deirdre O'Shea, and Stephen Gallagher, "Feeling Thanks and Saying Thanks: A Randomized Controlled Trial Examining If and How Socially Oriented Gratitude Journals

Work," *Journal of Clinical Psychology* 73, no. 10 (March 6, 2017): 1280–1300, https://doi.org/10.1002/jclp.22469.

28 **thanking someone mentioned in your gratitude journal:** Kira M. Newman, "How to Upgrade Your Gratitude Practice," *Greater Good Magazine*, April 4, 2017, https://greatergood.berkeley.edu/article/item/how_to_upgrade_your_gratitude _practice.

29 **multiple positive health benefits:** Rollin McCraty et al., "The Impact of a New Emotional Self-Management Program on Stress, Emotions, Heart Rate Variability, DHEA and Cortisol," *Integrative Physiological and Behavioral Science* 33, no. 2 (1998): 151–70, https://doi.org/10.1007/BF02688660; Fuschia M. Sirois and Alex M. Wood, "Gratitude Uniquely Predicts Lower Depression in Chronic Illness Populations: A Longitudinal Study of Inflammatory Bowel Disease and Arthritis," *Health Psychology* 36, no. 2 (2016): 122–32, https:// doi.org/10.1037/hea0000436; Marta Jackowska et al., "The Impact of a Brief Gratitude Intervention on Subjective Well-Being, Biology, and Sleep," *Journal of Health Psychology* 21, no. 10 (2016): 2207–17, https://doi.org/10.1177/1359 105315572455; Randolph Wolf Shipon, "Gratitude: Effect on Perspectives and Blood Pressure of Inner-City African-American Hypertensive Patients," *Dissertation Abstracts International: Section B: The Sciences and Engineering* 68, no. 3-B (2007): 1977; Laura S. Redwine et al., " Pilot Randomized Study of a Gratitude Journaling Intervention on HRV and Inflammatory Biomarkers in Stage B Heart Failure Patients," *Psychosomatic Medicine* 78, no. 6 (2016): 667–76, https://insights.ovid.com/crossref?an=00006842-201607000-00005; and Alex M. Wood et al., "Gratitude Influences Sleep Through the Mechanism of Pre-Sleep Cognitions," *Journal of Psychosomatic Research* 66, no. 1 (2009): 43–8, https://doi.org/10.1016/j.jpsychores.2008.09.002.

29 **science of gratitude:** "Gratitude Is Good Medicine," UC Davis Health Medical Center, November 25, 2015, https://health.ucdavis.edu/medicalcenter /features/2015-2016/11/20151125_gratitude.html.

29 **Stanford commencement address:** "Steve Jobs' 2005 Stanford Commencement Address," YouTube video, posted by Stanford, March 7, 2008, https://www.youtube.com/watch?v=UF8uR6Z6KLc; and Stanford Report, quoting Steve Jobs, "'You've Got to Find What You Love,' Jobs Says," *Stanford News*, June 14, 2005, https://news.stanford.edu/news/2005/june15/jobs -061505.html.

35 **psychologists and neuroscientists:** Multiple psychologists, neuroscientists, and others have studied happiness. Martin E. P. Seligman, a psychologist, author, and educator, is the godfather of what is known as positive psychology. Seligman and his colleagues have studied and written extensively about happiness, well-being, positive psychology, and learned helplessness, among other topics.

35 **happiness is the precursor to success:** Shawn Achor, *The Happiness Advantage* (New York: Crown, 2010), 3–4.

35 **the greatest competitive advantage:** Dan Schawbel, "Shawn Achor: What You Need to Do Before Experiencing Happiness," *Forbes*, September 10, 2013, https://www.forbes.com/sites/danschawbel/2013/09/10/shawn-achor-what-you-need-to-do-before-experiencing-happiness.

35 **a 31 percent increase in productivity:** Schawbel, "Shawn Achor."

35 **studies demonstrate that a positive effect:** Kathy Caprino, "How Happiness Directly Impacts Your Success," *Forbes*, June 6, 2013, https://www.forbes.com/sites/kathycaprino/2013/06/06/how-happiness-directly-impacts-your-success.

35 **Researchers Sonja Lyubomirsky, Laura King, and Ed Diener:** Sonja Lyubomirsky, Laura King, and Ed Diener, "The Benefits of Frequent Positive Affect: Does Happiness Lead to Success?" *Psychological Bulletin* 131, no. 6 (2005): 803–55, https://doi.org/10.1037/0033-2909.131.6.803.

35 **including career:** Julia K. Boehm and Sonja Lyubomirsky, "Does Happiness Promote Career Success?" *Journal of Career Assessment* 16, no. 1 (2008): 101–16, https://doi.org/10.1177/1069072707308140.

35 **happiness is the result of success:** Lisa C. Walsh, Julia K. Boehm, and Sonja Lyubomirsky, "Does Happiness Promote Career Success? Revisiting the Evidence," *Journal of Career Assessment* 26, no. 2 (2018): 199–219, https://doi.org/10.1177/1069072717751441.

36 **Lemonade Lifers think life works like this:** For more on happiness and life satisfaction, see Christopher Peterson, Nansook Park, and Martin E. P. Seligman, "Orientations to Happiness and Life Satisfaction: The Full Life Versus the Empty Life," *Journal of Happiness Studies* 6, no. 1 (2005): 25–41, https://doi.org/10.1007/s10902-004-1278-z; and Sonja Lyubomirsky, Kennon M. Sheldon, and Schkade, "Pursuing Happiness: The Architecture of Sustainable Change," *Review of General Psychology* 9, no. 2 (2005): 111–31, http://dx.doi.org/10.1037/1089-2680.9.2.111.

36 **When you're happy today:** This is based on the work of Seligman, Achor, Lyubomirsky, King, Diener, and others whose research has shown that happiness yields success and that the traditional success-happiness model is incomplete or backward. Lemonade Lifers believe that happiness starts today, and by embracing happiness, they create positive results in their life.

37 **according to psychologists Tara Kraft and Sarah Pressman:** Tara L. Kraft and Sarah D. Pressman, "Grin and Bear It: The Influence of Manipulated Facial Expression on the Stress Response," *Psychological Science* 23, no. 11 (2012): 1372–78, https://doi.org/10.1177/0956797612445312.

37 **Seven Wonders of the Ancient World:** Joshua J. Mark, "The Seven Wonders," *Ancient History Encyclopedia*, September 2, 2009, https://www.ancient.eu/The_Seven_Wonders/.

38 gratitude, which is strongly associated with more happiness: Robert A. Emmons and Cheryl A. Crumpler, "Gratitude as a Human Strength: Appraising the Evidence," *Journal of Social and Clinical Psychology* 19, no. 1 (2000): 56–69, https://doi.org/10.1521/jscp.2000.19.1.56.

38 Researchers at Cornell University: Amit Kumar, Matthew A. Killingsworth, and Thomas Gilovich, "Waiting for Merlot Anticipatory Consumption of Experiential and Material Purchases," *Psychological Science* 25, no. 10 (2014):1924–31, https://doi.org/10.1177/0956797614546556.

38 Commit acts of kindness: Keiko Atake et al., "Happy People Become Happier Through Kindness: A Counting Kindness Intervention," *Journal of Happiness Studies* 7, no. 3 (2006): 361–65, https://doi.org/10.1007/s10902-005 -3650-z.

38 pay for the person behind you: Elizabeth W. Dunn, Lara B. Aknin, and Michael I. Norton, "Spending Money on Others Promotes Happiness," *Science* 319, no. 5870 (2008):1687–88, http://science.sciencemag.org/content/319/5870/1687.

39 the joy of giving outlasts the joy of receiving: Ed O'Brien and Samantha Kassirer, "People Are Slow to Adapt to the Warm Glow of Giving," *Psychological Science*, 2018, https://doi.org/10.1177/0956797618814145.

39 hedonic adaptation: O'Brien and Kassirer, "People Are Slow to Adapt."

39 In one experiment, researchers gave participants: O'Brien and Kassirer, "People Are Slow to Adapt."

39 Dolly Parton's father: Dolly Parton, "Letter from Dolly," Imagination Library, https://imaginationlibrary.com/letter-from-dolly/.

40 The Imagination Library delivers: Maureen Pao, "Dolly Parton Gives the Gift of Literacy: A Library of 100 Million Books," nprED, March 1, 2018, https://www.npr.org/sections/ed/2018/03/01/589912466/dolly-parton-gives -the-gift-of-literacy-a-library-of-100-million-books.

CHAPTER 4: ESCAPE THE CHASM OF CAN'T

46 you're the average of the five people: Aimee Groth, "You're the Average of the Five People You Spend the Most Time With," *Business Insider*, July 24, 2012, http://www.businessinsider.com/jim-rohn-youre-the-average-of-the-five-people -you-spend-the-most-time-with-2012-7.

46 your most important group of influencers: Sigal G. Barsade, "The Ripple Effect: Emotional Contagion and Its Influence on Group Behavior," *Administrative Science Quarterly* 47, no. 4 (2002): 644–75, http://dx.doi.org/10.2139/ssrn.250894.

46 A metastudy of more than three hundred thousand adults: Julianne Holt- Lunstad, Timothy B. Smith, and J. Bradley Layton, "Social Relationships and Mortality Risk: A Meta-Analytic Review," *PLOS Medicine* 7, no. 7 (2010): e1000316, https://doi.org/10.1371/journal.pmed.1000316.

46 increase your longevity by 50 percent: Katherine Harmon, "Social Ties Boost Survival by 50 Percent," *Scientific American*, July 28, 2010, https://www .scientificamerican.com/article/relationships-boost-survival/.

46 having the wrong wolfpack: Erin Hutkin, "Unhealthy Relationships Cause Unhealthy Bodies," *San Diego Union-Tribune*, September 23, 2014, https://www .sandiegouniontribune.com/news/health/sdut-unhealthy-relationships-unhealthy -bodies-2014sep23-htmlstory.html; and Theresa Tamkins, "Unhappily Ever After: Why Bad Marriages Hurt Women's Health," CNN, March 6, 2009, http://www.cnn.com/2009/HEALTH/03/06/marriage.women.heart/index.html.

49 When Jim Carrey: "What Oprah Learned from Jim Carrey," Oprah's Life Class/Oprah Winfrey Network, YouTube video from February 17, 1997 interview, posted October 12, 2011, by OWN, https://www.youtube.com /watch?v=nPU5bjzLZX0.

49 Well, I do have these [roles]: "What Oprah Learned."

50 a $20 million advance: Richard Natale, "Is Rich and Richer Dumb and Dumber?: Movies: Jim Carrey's $20-Million Fee for 'The Cable Guy' Alarms Some in the Industry, While His Managers Call It a 'Genius' Move by Sony," *Los Angeles Times*, June 22, 1995, http://articles.latimes.com/1995-06-22/entertainment /ca-15726_1_jim-carrey.

52 James Dyson spent fifteen years: Nadia Goodman, "James Dyson on Using Failure to Drive Success," *Entrepreneur*, November 5, 2012, https://www .entrepreneur.com/article/224855.

52 iterative process: Madison Malone-Kircher, "James Dyson on 5,126 Vacuums That Didn't Work—and the One That Finally Did," *New York*, November 22, 2016, http://nymag.com/vindicated/2016/11/james-dyson-on -5–126-vacuums-that-didnt-work-and-1-that-did.html.

53 the store's annual revenue from $72,000 to $250,000: Nicholas Graves, "1945: Sam Walton Buys His First Store," The Walmart Digital Museum, https://walmartmuseum.auth.cap-hosting.com/blog/1945_sam_walton_buys _his_first_store/.

53 lease didn't have a renewal clause: Samuel Moore Walton with John Huey, *Sam Walton: Made in America* (New York: Doubleday, 1992).

54 which caused shoppers to spend more money: Sandra S. Vance and Roy V. Scott, *Wal-Mart: A History of Sam Walton's Retail Phenomenon*, Twayne's Evolution of Modern Business Series, no. 11 (New York: Twayne, 1994), 11–12.

54 to reduce payroll costs: Richard S. Tedlow, *Giants of Enterprise: Seven Business Innovators and the Empires They Built* (New York: HarperBusiness, 2001), 315–86.

54 Nineteen years after Walton left town: Tedlow, *Giants of Enterprise*, 335.

CHAPTER 5: EMBRACE THE REWARDS OF RISK

61 **Be Like the Guy Who Invented the Lollipop Stick Machine:** Alana Horowitz, "The Unknown Geniuses Behind 10 of the Most Useful Inventions Ever," *Business Insider*, March 3, 2011, http://www.businessinsider.com/ten -inventions-you-never-knew-had-inventors-2011-3.

62 **Ernie Fraze:** "Ermal Fraze," Ohio History Central, http://www.ohiohistory central.org/w/Ermal_Fraze; "Ermal Fraze," Lemelson-MIT, https://lemelson.mit .edu/resources/ermal-fraze.

62 **Sam Born:** "Our History," Just Born website, accessed March 1, 2019, https://www.justborn.com/who-we-are/our-history.

63 **Hymen Lipman:** Pagan Kennedy, "Who Made That Built-In Eraser?" *New York Times*, September 13, 2013, https://www.nytimes.com/2013/09/15 /magazine/who-made-that-built-in-eraser.html.

63 **In 1875, the US Supreme Court ruled:** Reckendorfer v. Faber, 92 U.S. 347 (1875).

63 **Charles Brannock:** "About Us," Brannock website, https://brannock.com/pages /about-us.

64 **Bette Nesmith Graham:** "Bette Nesmith Graham," Lemelson-MIT, https://lemelson.mit.edu/resources/bette-nesmith-graham.

CHAPTER 6: YOUR CAREER DEPENDS ON THE GREEK ALPHABET

73 **Jack Ma was a teacher:** "Jack Ma's Interview with Charlie Rose, 2015," World Economic Forum, YouTube video, posted by Alibaba Group, January 28, 2015, https://www.youtube.com/watch?v=LWgwApN_Ef8.

74 **But Ma understood how to seize opportunities:** Calum MacLeod, "Alibaba's Jack Ma: From 'Crazy' to China's Richest Man," *USA Today*, September 17, 2004, https://www.usatoday.com/story/tech/2014/09/17/alibaba-jack-ma -profile/15406641/; and Jillian D'Onfro, "How Jack Ma Went from Being a Poor School Teacher to Turning Alibaba into a $168 Billion Behemoth," *Business Insider*, May 7, 2014, http://www.businessinsider.com/jack-ma-founder-alibaba -2014-5.

75 **In the mid-1960s, Don Fisher:** "Don Fisher, 1928–2009," Gap website, http://www.gapinc.com/content/dam/gapincsite/documents/DonFisher_Bio. pdf; and "Doris and Donald Fisher," California Museum, accessed March 1, 2019, http://www.californiamuseum.org/inductee/doris-donald-fisher.

76 **Lawrence Wien:** Deirdre Carmody, "A Philanthropist Leaves His Mark," *New York Times*, August 8, 1982, http://www.nytimes.com/1982/08/09 /nyregion/a-philanthropist-leaves-his-mark.html; and Alfonso A. Narvaez, "Lawrence A. Wien, 83, Is Dead; and Lawyer Gave Millions to Charity," *New*

York Times, December 12, 1988, http://www.nytimes.com/1988/12/12
/obituaries/lawrence-a-wien-83-is-dead-lawyer-gave-millions-to-charity.html.

82 **about half of all managers don't trust their leaders:** Robert F. Hurley, "The
Decision to Trust," *Harvard Business Review*, September 2006, https://hbr.org
/2006/09/the-decision-to-trust.

82 **Your leadership approach doesn't have to mirror your boss's:** Shannon
G. Taylor et al., "Does Having a Bad Boss Make You More Likely to Be One
Yourself?" *Harvard Business Review*, January 23, 2019, https://hbr.org/2019/01
/does-having-a-bad-boss-make-you-more-likely-to-be-one-yourself.

82 **financial consequences for organizations:** Michael Housman and Dylan
Minor, "Toxic Workers," Working Paper 16–057, *Harvard Business School*, 2015,
https://news.harvard.edu/wp-content/uploads/2015/11/16-057_d45c0b4f-fa19
-49de-8f1b-4b12fe054fea.pdf.

82 **Research shows that incivility at work:** Christine Porath and Christine
Pearson, "The Price of Incivility," *Harvard Business Review*, January–February
2013, https://hbr.org/2013/01/the-price-of-incivility.

90 **In his farewell speech:** Richard Nixon, "President Richard Nixon's Final
Remarks at The White House" (speech, Washington, DC, August 9, 1974), CNN,
http://www.cnn.com/ALLPOLITICS/1997/gen/resources/watergate/nixon.farewell
.html.

95 **You can create meaning at work:** Monique Valcour, "Make Your Work
More Meaningful," *Harvard Business Review*, August 16, 2013, https://hbr.org
/2013/08/make-your-work-more-meaningful.

97 **lottery for *Hamilton* tickets:** Kelli B. Grant, "*Hamilton* Tony Nods May
Make Getting Tix Even Harder," CNBC, May 2, 2016, https://www.cnbc.com
/2016/05/02/getting-hamilton-tickets-takes-patience-and-money.html.

97 **Jeff Bezos sitting at his first desk, which was literally a door:** Ali Montag,
"Jeff Bezos' First Desk at Amazon Was a Door with Four-by-Fours for Legs—
Here's Why It Still Is Today," CNBC, January 23, 2018, https://www.cnbc.com
/2018/01/23/jeff-bezos-first-desk-at-amazon-was-made-of-a-wooden-door.html;
and Jillian D'Onfro and Eugene Kim, "The Life and Awesomeness of Amazon
Founder and CEO Jeff Bezos," CNBC, February 11, 2016, http://www
.businessinsider.com/the-life-of-amazon-founder-ceo-jeff-bezos-2014-7.

98 **I want you to meet Brian:** Brian Chesky, "7 Rejections," Medium, July 12,
2015, https://medium.com/@bchesky/7-rejections-7d894cbaa084.

99 **Kevin O'Leary, *Shark Tank*'s Mr. Wonderful:** "Kevin O'Leary's Story"
(interview on *Dragon's Den*), YouTube video, posted on April 20, 2013, https://
www.youtube.com/watch?v=mnCmmHs_XO8.

99 **"Within minutes, I was on my bicycle:** "Kevin O'Leary's Story."

99 **Years later, with cofounder Michael Perik:** Kevin O'Leary, "Shark Tank

Investor Kevin O'Leary Explains How a $10,000 Loan from His Mother Helped Him Build a $4 Billion Company," *Business Insider*, April 17, 2015, http://www.businessinsider.com/the-best-money-kevin-oleary-ever-spent-2015-4; and Lawrence M. Fisher, "Mattel Decides to Put on Sale Software Unit Bought in May," *New York Times*, April 4, 2000, https://www.nytimes.com/2000/04/04/business/mattel-decides-to-put-on-sale-software-unit-bought-in-may.html.

99 **Mattel acquired the Learning Company:** Catherine Clifford, "Shark Tank Star Kevin O'Leary: There's 'Not a Chance in Hell' I Will Invest in Your Start-Up If You Still Have a Day Job," CNBC, June 15, 2017, https://www.cnbc.com/2017/06/15/shark-tank-star-kevin-oleary-wont-invest-in-founders-with-day-jobs.html.

CHAPTER 7: HOW TO MAKE $110,237 IN LESS THAN ONE HOUR

103 **recognize patterns that helps us to read:** Gary Everding, "Children's Learning to Spell, Read Aided by Pattern Recognition, Use," The Source, Washington University in St. Louis, April 25, 2003, https://source.wustl.edu/2003/04/children-learning-to-spell-read-aided-by-pattern-recognition-use/.

103 **understand language:** Evan Kidd and Joanne Arciuli, "Individual Differences in Statistical Learning Predict Children's Comprehension of Syntax," *Child Development* 87, no. 1 (2016): 184, https://doi.org/10.1111/cdev.12461.

103 **learn music:** Mark P. Matson, "Superior Pattern Processing Is the Essence of the Evolved Human Brain," *Frontiers in Neuroscience* 8, no. 265 (2014), https://doi.org/10.3389/fnins.2014.00265.

103 **recognize familiar faces:** Knvul Sheikh, "How We Save Face—Researchers Crack the Brain's Facial-Recognition Code," *Scientific American*, June 1, 2017, https://www.scientificamerican.com/article/how-we-save-face-researchers-crack-the-brains-facial-recognition-code/; and R. Jenkins, A. J. Dowsett, and A. M. Burton, "How Many Faces Do People Know?" *Proceedings of the Royal Society B: Biological Sciences* 285, no. 1888 (2018), https://doi.org/10.1098/rspb.2018.1319.

103 **we can complete a sequence like the alphabet:** Yusef Perwej and Ashish Chaturvedi, "Neural Networks for Handwritten English Alphabet Recognition," *International Journal of Computer Applications* 20, no. 7 (April 2011), https://arxiv.org/ftp/arxiv/papers/1205/1205.3966.pdf.

103 **an ice cream truck driver from Ohio named Michael Larson:** Garin Pirnia, "11 Whammy-Free Facts About *Press Your Luck*," *Mental Floss*, September 26, 2016, http://mentalfloss.com/article/76656/11-whammy-free-facts-about-press-your-luck.

103 *Press Your Luck* **was a daytime game show:** "*Press Your Luck*," IMDB, accessed March 1, 2019, https://www.imdb.com/title/tt0136655/.

104 **Of the show's more than seven hundred episodes:** "*Press Your Luck*."

104 **So, how did he do it?:** *Big Bucks: The Press Your Luck Scandal*, television documentary, directed by James P. Taylor Jr. (Los Angeles, CA: GSN, 2003); Zachary Crockett, "The Man Who Got No Whammies," Priceonomics, September 14, 2015, https://priceonomics.com/the-man-who-got-no-whammies/; and Chris Higgins, "The Man Who Pressed His Luck . . . and Won," *Mental Floss*, May 7, 2013, http://mentalfloss.com/article/28588/man-who-pressed-his-luckand-won; "*Press Your Luck* Michael Larson Parts 1 & 2 (Full Credits)," broadcasted by KTXH-DT 20, July 31, 2016, video posted by Jordan Baker, August 1, 2016, https://www.youtube.com/watch?v=WltjaxiowW4.

105 **The underlying science works like this:** Kyle S. Smith and Ann M. Graybiel, "Habit Formation," *Dialogues in Clinical Neuroscience* 18, no. 1 (2016): 33–43, https://www.ncbi.nlm.nih.gov/pmc/articles/PMC4826769/.

105 **The secret to breaking a bad habit:** Kyle S. Smith et al., "Reversible Online Control of Habitual Behavior by Optogenetic Perturbation of Medial Prefrontal Cortex," *Proceedings of the National Academy of Sciences* 109, no. 46 (2012): 18932–37, https://doi.org/10.1073/pnas.1216264109.

105 **In *The Power of Habit*:** Charles Duhigg, *The Power of Habit: Why We Do What We Do In Life* (New York: Random House, 2012).

106 **you can learn how to change bad habits:** Robert Taibbi, "How to Break Bad Habits," *Psychology Today*, December 15, 2017, https://www.psychology today.com/us/blog/fixing-families/201712/how-break-bad-habits.

106 **the why behind the behavior:** William James, *The Principles of Psychology*, vol. 1 (New York: Cosimo, 1890).

107 **Judge Judy:** "Judge Judy's Bio," Judge Judy website, accessed March 1, 2019, http://www.judgejudy.com/bios.

108 **psychologist Solomon Asch:** Solomon E. Asch, "Studies of Independence and Conformity: I. A Minority of One Against a Unanimous Majority," *Psychological Monographs: General and Applied* 70, no. 9 (1956): 1–70, http://dx.doi.org/10.1037/h0093718; Solomon E. Asch, "Opinions and Social Pressure," *Scientific American* 193, no. 5 (1955): 31–5, http://dx.doi.org/10.1038/scientificamerican1155-31; and Saul McLeod, "Solomon Asch—Conformity Experiment," *Simply Psychology*, updated December 28, 2018, https://www.simplypsychology.org/asch-conformity.html.

108 **Asch found that across multiple clinical trials:** McLeod, "Solomon Asch."

108 **normative influence:** Erin L. Mead et al., "Understanding the Sources of Normative Influence on Behavior: The Example of Tobacco," *Social Science & Medicine* 115 (2014): 139–43, https://doi.org/10.1016/j.socscimed.2014.05.030.

108 informational influence: Morton Deutsch and Harold B. Gerard, "A Study of Normative and Informational Social Influences upon Individual Judgment," *Journal of Abnormal and Social Psychology* 51, no. 3 (1955): 629–36, http://dx .doi.org/10.1037/h0046408.

109 *12 Angry Men*: *12 Angry Men*, film, directed by Sidney Lumet (Los Angeles, CA: United Artists, 1957).

109 The next time you're in that meeting: James R. Detert, "Cultivating Everyday Courage," *Harvard Business Review*, November–December 2018, https://hbr.org/2018/11/cultivating-everyday-courage.

109 goodwill and credibility with your colleagues: Detert, "Cultivating Everyday Courage."

111 Norwegian-American sociologist and economist: Thorstein Veblen, *The Theory of the Leisure Class: An Economic Study of Institutions* (New York: Macmillan, 1899).

111 Arthur R. ("Pop") Momand created the phrase: William Safire, "On Language; Up the Down Ladder," *New York Times Magazine*, November 15, 1998, https://www.nytimes.com/1998/11/15/magazine/on-language-up-the -down-ladder.html.

111 Keeping up with the Joneses: Don Markstein, "Keeping Up with the Joneses," Toonopedia, 2002, http://www.toonopedia.com/joneses.htm.

113 Daddy Warbucks: Don Markstein, "Little Orphan Annie," Toonopedia, http://www.toonopedia.com/annie.htm.

114 Appearances can be deceiving: Mihaly Csikszentmihalyi, "If We Are So Rich, Why Aren't We Happy?" *American Psychologist* 54, no. 10 (1999): 821–27, http://dx.doi.org/10.1037/0003-066X.54.10.821.

CHAPTER 8: TAKE IT PERSONALLY

119 a bronze statue of John Harvard: "Historical Facts," Harvard University, accessed March 1, 2019, https://www.harvard.edu/about-harvard/harvard -glance/history/historical-facts.

119 the Statue of Three Lies: "The 3 Lies of Harvard," Harvard University, accessed March 1, 2019, https://www.summer.harvard.edu/inside-summer /3-lies-harvard.

119 Harvard is the oldest institution: "University Rankings: World's Top 20 Universities," *Telegraph*, June 23, 2017, https://www.telegraph.co.uk/education /0/revealed-worlds-top-20-universities.

120 John Harvard bequeathed: Jennifer Tomase, "Tale of John Harvard's Surviving Book," *Harvard Gazette*, November 1, 2007, https://news.harvard.edu /gazette/story/2007/11/tale-of-john-harvards-surviving-book/.

120 **died from tuberculosis:** Tomase, "Tale of John Harvard's."

120 **French used a model—Sherman Hoar:** Sebastian Smee, "Before He Sculped Lincoln," *Boston Globe*, October 27, 2016, https://www.bostonglobe.com/arts/art/2016/10/26/before-sculpted-lincoln/Op5dJrjLt0RdQRVkPc0TsJ/story.html.

124 **Don't take it personally:** F. Diane Barth, "Don't Take It Personally," *Psychology Today*, July 3, 2010, https://www.psychologytoday.com/us/blog/the-couch/201007/dont-take-it-personally.

125 **Berthold der Schwarze:** Michael Jinkins, "The Mirror Test," Louisville Seminary, May 27, 2014, http://www.lpts.edu/about/our-leadership/president/thinking-out-loud/thinking-out-loud/2014/05/27/the-mirror-test (page no longer available).

125 **one of the greatest corporate turnarounds in history:** Bill Taylor, "How Domino's Pizza Reinvented Itself," *Harvard Business Review*, November 28, 2016, https://hbr.org/2016/11/how-dominos-pizza-reinvented-itself.

125 **In unconventional fashion:** Adam Sternbergh, "The Art of the Apology Ad," *New Republic*, August 3, 2010, https://newrepublic.com/article/76719/art-apology-ad-bp-toyota-dominos.

125 **Doyle ran advertisements:** Paul Farhi, "Behind Domino's Mea Culpa Ad Campaign," *Washington Post*, January 13, 2010.

126 **The SWOT analysis:** Albert Humphrey, "SWOT Analysis for Management Consulting," *SRI Alumni Newsletter*, 7–8, 2005.

127 **the centerpiece should be your strengths:** Peter F. Drucker, "On Managing Oneself," in *HBR's 10 Must Reads On Managing Yourself* (Cambridge: Harvard Business School Press, 2010), 13–32.

128 **feedback analysis:** Drucker, "On Managing Oneself"; and Joe Maciariello, "Joe's Journal: Feedback Through the Ages," Drucker Institute, January 31, 2012, http://www.druckerinstitute.com/2012/01/feedback-through-the-ages/.

131 **In New York City:** Mindy Fetterman, "Seeking a Quiet Place in a Nation of Noise," *The Pew Charitable Trusts* (blog), April 16, 2018, http://www.pewtrusts.org/en/research-and-analysis/blogs/stateline/2018/04/16/seeking-a-quiet-place-in-a-nation-of-noise.

131 **In midtown Manhattan:** Fetterman, "Seeking a Quiet Place."

132 **the European Union:** Fetterman, "Seeking a Quiet Place."

CHAPTER 9: ALWAYS TAKE NO FOR AN ANSWER

137 **never take no for an answer:** Winston Churchill, *My Early Life: A Roving Commission* (London: Thornton Butterworth, 1930), 60.

137 **never give up and to keep pushing:** Harvey Deutschendorf, "7 Habits of Highly Persistent People," *Fast Company*, April 1, 2015, https://www.fastcompany.com/3044531/7-habits-of-highly-persistent-people; Glen Geher, "5 Reasons You Should Never Give Up," *Psychology Today*, March 4, 2015, https://

www.psychologytoday.com/us/blog/darwins-subterranean-world/201503/5
-reasons-you-should-never-give.

137 **just ask Ray Kroc:** Ray Kroc, *Grinding It Out: The Making of McDonald's*
(New York: St. Martin's Press, 1977); Eric Pace, "Ray A. Kroc dies at 81; Built
McDonald's Chain," *New York Times*, January 5, 1984, https://archive.nytimes
.com/www.nytimes.com/learning/general/onthisday/bday/1005.html; and "Ray
Kroc," *Entrepreneur*, October 9, 2008, https://www.entrepreneur.com/article
/197544.

138 **Unlike the traditional drive-in restaurant:** "Our History," McDonald's,
accessed March 1, 2019, https://www.mcdonalds.com/us/en-us/about-us/our
-history.html.

141 **Have a "can-do" attitude:** Annabelle Thorpe, "How to . . . Develop a Can-
do Attitude," *Guardian*, May 5, 2001, https://www.theguardian.com/money
/2001/may/05/jobsadvice.careers2.

141 **being honest with yourself:** Celia Moore et al., "The Advantage of Being
Oneself: The Role of Applicant Self-Verification in Organizational Hiring
Decisions," *Journal of Applied Psychology* 102, no. 11 (2017): 1493–1513,
http://dx.doi.org/10.1037/apl0000223.

142 **self-verification:** Moore et al., "The Advantage of Being Oneself."

142 **negative self-views:** Henry Bodkin, "Being Honest About Weaknesses Is
Key to Landing Top Jobs, New Study Finds," *Telegraph*, June 22, 2017, https://
www.telegraph.co.uk/science/2017/06/22/honest-weaknesses-key-landing-top
-jobs-new-study-finds/.

142 **Previous research has shown:** Julia Levashina and Michael A. Campion,
"Measuring Faking in the Employment Interview: Development and Validation
of an Interview Faking Behavior Scale," *Journal of Applied Psychology* 92, no. 6
(2007): 1638–56, https://psycnet.apa.org/doiLanding?doi=10.1037%2F0021-90
10.92.6.1638.

144 **negativity bias:** Tiffany A. Ito et al., "Negative Information Weighs More
Heavily on the Brain: The Negativity Bias in Evaluative Categorizations," *Journal
of Personality and Social Psychology* 75, no. 4 (1998): 887–900, http://dx.doi.org
/10.1037/0022-3514.75.4.887.

149 **a life purpose can help you outlive your peers:** Patrick L. Hill and Nicholas
A. Turiano, "Purpose in Life as a Predictor of Mortality Across Adulthood,"
Psychological Science 25, no. 7 (2014): 1482–86, https://doi.org/10.1177
/0956797614531799.

149 **People with a sense of purpose also report:** Patrick L. Hill et al., "The
Value of a Purposeful Life: Sense of Purpose Predicts Greater Income and Net
Worth," *Journal of Research in Personality* 65 (2016): 38–42, https://doi.org
/10.1016/j.jrp.2016.07.003.

150 **When you combine your unique gifts:** Martin E. P. Seligman, *Authentic Happiness: Using the New Positive Psychology to Realize Your Potential for Lasting Fulfillment* (New York: Free Press, 2002), 249.

CHAPTER 10: NEVER HAVE A BACKUP PLAN

157 **it's common wisdom:** Mariana Simoes, "Instant MBA: Always Have a Back Up Plan," *Business Insider*, March 19, 2013, https://www.businessinsider.com /always-have-a-plan-b-2013-3.

158 **ditch your backup plan:** Jihae Shin and Katherine L. Milkman, "How Backup Plans Can Harm Goal Pursuit: The Unexpected Downside of Being Prepared for Failure," *Organizational Behavior and Human Decision Processes* 135 (2016): 1–9, https://doi.org/10.1016/j.obhdp.2016.04.003.

159 **Professors Katherine Milkman and Jihae Shin:** Katherine Milkman and Jihae Shin, "Having a 'Plan B' Can Hurt Your Chances of Success," *Scientific American*, July 19, 2016, https://www.scientificamerican.com/article/having-a -plan-b-can-hurt-your-chances-of-success.

160 **An episode of *Oprah*:** "Tyler Perry Biography," Biography.com, updated January 31, 2019, https://www.biography.com/people/tyler-perry-361274.

160 **Tyler Perry:** "Tyler Perry Biography"; "The Many Faces of Tyler Perry," CBN, accessed March 1, 2019, http://www1.cbn.com/700club/many-faces -tyler-perry; and "Tyler Perry—Success with Plays," Biography.com, accessed March 1, 2019, https://www.biography.com/video/tyler-perry-success-with -plays-14938179730.

161 **Sylvester Stallone:** "'Rocky Isn't Based on Me,' Says Stallone, 'but We Both Went the Distance,'" *New York Times*, November 1, 1976, https://archive.nytimes .com/www.nytimes.com/packages/html/movies/bestpictures/rocky-ar.html; "The Rocky Story by Sly part 1 of 4," interview, YouTube video, posted by Michael Watson, December 8, 2007, https://www.youtube.com/watch?v=PJvPD2u3YBI; Tom Ward, "The Amazing Story of the Making of *Rocky*," *Forbes*, August 29, 2017, https://www.forbes.com/sites/tomward/2017/08/29/the-amazing-story-of -the-making-of-rocky/; Eric Raskin, "'Real Rocky' Wepner Finally Getting Due," ESPN.com, October 25, 2011, http://www.espn.com/boxing/story/_/page /IamChuckWepner/chuck-wepner-recognized-rocky-fame; "The Rocky Story Part 1 of 9," YouTube video, posted by Michael Watson, January 3, 2012, https://www.youtube.com/watch?v=IAsACXArEc4; and Chris Nashawaty, "How Rocky Nabbed Best Picture," *Entertainment Weekly*, February 19, 2002, http:// ew.com/article/2002/02/19/how-rocky-nabbed-best-picture/.

164 **"Dixie cup" hat:** United States Naval Academy Public Affairs Office, "History and Traditions of the Herndon Monument Climb," USNA website, accessed March 1, 2019, https://www.usna.edu/PAO/faq_pages/herndon.php.

164 **Herndon Monument:** Dan Zak, "The Shirtless Monument Climb at the Naval Academy Is America's Best Spectator Sport," *Washington Post*, May 23, 2016, https://www.washingtonpost.com/news/arts-and-entertainment/wp/2016/05/23/the-shirtless-monument-climb-at-the-naval-academy-is-americas-best-spectator-sport/.

167 **Work backward from your goal:** Jooyoung Park, Lu Fang-Chi, and William Hedgecock, "Relative Effects of Forward and Backward Planning on Goal Pursuit," *Psychological Science* 28, no. 11 (2017): 1620–30, https://doi.org/10.1177/0956797617715510.

167 **begin with the customer experience and work backward to the technology:** Steve Jobs, "Business Strategy: Start with Your Customer and Work Backwards to a Product or Service," from Apple World Wide Developers Conference, 1997, video, August 6, 2017, https://www.youtube.com/watch?v=48j493tfO-o.

167 **reverse engineer:** Daniel Lyons, "We Start with the Customer and We Work Backward," *Slate*, December 24, 2009, https://slate.com/news-and-politics/2009/12/jeff-bezos-on-amazon-s-success.html.

CHAPTER 11: IGNORE THE SHORTEST DISTANCE

171 **Greek mathematician Archimedes:** Robert Tubbs, *What Is a Number? Mathematical Concepts and Their Origins* (Baltimore: Johns Hopkins University Press, 2009), 159–60.

174 **Meet Harland:** Harland Sanders, *Col. Harland Sanders: The Autobiography of the Original Celebrity Chef* (Louisville: KFC Corporation, 2012); and William Whitworth, "Kentucky Fried," *New Yorker*, February 14, 1970, https://www.newyorker.com/magazine/1970/02/14/kentucky-fried.

175 **trailblazers who all made it big after age forty:** Richard Feloni, "24 People Who Became Highly Successful after Age 40," *Business Insider*, June 23, 2015, http://www.businessinsider.com/24-people-who-became-highly-successful-after-age-40-2015-6.

175 **more than 120 movies:** Seth Abramovitch, "120 Movies, $13 Billion in Box Office: How Samuel L. Jackson Became Hollywood's Most Bankable Star," *Hollywood Reporter*, January 9, 2019, https://www.hollywoodreporter.com/features/how-samuel-l-jackson-became-hollywoods-bankable-star-1174613.

176 *On the Origin of Species***:** Charles Darwin, *On the Origin of Species* (London: John Murray, 1859).

184 **The Evolution of the Straw:** Derek Thompson, "The Amazing History and the Strange Invention of the Bendy Straw," *Atlantic*, November 22, 2011, https://www.theatlantic.com/business/archive/2011/11/the-amazing-history-and-the-strange-invention-of-the-bendy-straw/248923/; Kat Eschner, "Why You Should Appreciate the Invention of the Bendy Straw," *Smithsonian.com*,

September 28, 2017, https://www.smithsonianmag.com/smart-news/why
-appreciate-bendy-straw-180965014/; Alexis Madrigal, "Disposable America,"
Atlantic, June 21, 2018, https://www.theatlantic.com/technology/archive
/2018/06/disposable-america/563204/; Catherine Hollander, "A Brief History
of the Straw," *Bon Appétit*, October 23, 2014, http://www.bonappetit.com
/entertaining-style/trends-news/article/history-of-the-straw; and "The Straight
Truth about the Flexible Drinking Straw," Lemelson Center for the Study
of Invention and Automation, Smithsonian National Museum of American
History, June 1, 2002, http://invention.si.edu/straight-truth-about-flexible
-drinking-straw.

CONCLUSION

197 Edmund Hillary: Dennis McClellan, "Edmund Hillary, First to Climb Mt.
Everest, Dies," *Los Angeles Times*, January 11, 2008, http://www.latimes.com
/local/obituaries/la-me-hillary11jan11-story.html; "Sir Edmund Hillary:
Mountaineer Who Conquered Everest and Devoted His Later Life to the
Sherpa People of Nepal," *Independent*, January 12, 2008, https://www
.independent.co.uk/news/obituaries/sir-edmund-hillary-mountaineer-who
-conquered-everest-and-devoted-his-later-life-to-the-sherpa-people-769765
.html; Jennifer Latson, "The Low-Profile Pair Who Conquered Everest," *Time*,
May 29, 2015, http://time.com/3891554/hillary-norgay-everest-history;
"Edmund Hillary," Biography.com, updated February 20, 2016, https://www
.biography.com/people/edmund-hillary-9339111; and "Sir Edmund Hillary,"
Academy of Achievement, last revised February 6, 2019, http://www
.achievement.org/achiever/sir-edmund-hillary.

INDEX

ABOUT THE AUTHOR

Zack Friedman is the founder and chief executive officer of Make Lemonade, a leading personal finance company that empowers you to live a better financial life. He is an in-demand speaker and has inspired millions through his powerful insights, including more than fourteen million who have read his advice in *Forbes*. Previously, he was chief financial officer of an international energy company, was a hedge fund investor, and worked at Blackstone, Morgan Stanley, and the White House. Zack holds degrees from Harvard, Wharton, Columbia, and Johns Hopkins. He lives in New York with his wife and children.

Website: www.zackfriedman.com
Twitter: @zackafriedman
Facebook: /zackafriedman
Instagram: /zackafriedman

ABOUT MAKE LEMONADE

make lem●nade
Live a better financial life

WWW.MAKELEMONADE.CO

Make Lemonade is a leading personal finance company that empowers you to live a better financial life. Make Lemonade helps you find and compare the lowest rates and best deals on credit cards, student loans, personal loans, investing, banking, and more through free comparison tools, financial content, and product reviews.